Century in my Pocket is a delightful book. John Gilbert has written from the beginning of his life which has spanned the enormous changes of the twentieth century.

Everyone likes to know the little things about people. What they have done, who they have met and what they thought about the people they met.

This book is a most unusual account not only of the past, but up to the present day.

Dame Barbara Cartland
November, 1997

CENTURY
IN MY POCKET

John Gilbert

MINERVA PRESS
LONDON
MONTREUX   LOS ANGELES   SYDNEY

CENTURY IN MY POCKET
Copyright © John Gilbert 1998

ISBN 1 86106 337 7

First Published 1998 by
MINERVA PRESS
195 Knightsbridge
London SW7 1RE

Printed in Great Britain for Minerva Press

CENTURY
IN MY POCKET

For my mother,
who suffered so much but never complained, and who guided me
through my early life, always kind, gentle and helpful.

And for my wife Millie,
my loving companion, who was always there waiting for me on
my return at the end of each day.

Acknowledgements

My thanks are due to my friends, Irene Panter, who produced the text and illustrations and Patrick Cornes, who provided additional material for this book.

Contents

List of Illustrations

Chapter One
How Now Brown Cow?

Queen Victoria and cows dominated my life as a child.

Although I was born the year after Victoria's death in 1901, her influence lingered on in our home, and everything around us, as no doubt, it did in everyone else's. It was evident in the heavy furniture, the restrictive clothes, the aspidistras, the respect for class distinction, and, particularly as far as I was concerned, in the rules and regulations concerning the raising of a child. But above all, in Victoria's reign the work ethic was inculcated in each and every one of us, though in point of fact it didn't need much boosting, as poverty and hunger, grim parents of many a fatal infection, were always at our backs carrying the message: if you don't work, you don't eat.

From the Protestant work ethic sprang the entrepreneurial ideal, which I imbibed from childhood. Wasn't it constantly drummed into me, from the moment I can remember, that Great Britain was the great go-getting, engineering, inventive nation, with the words 'success' and 'administrative ability' engraved on the hearts of all her subjects?

Admittedly, with Victoria gone and Edward VII and the beautiful Queen Alexandra on the throne, an air, albeit illusory, of prosperity settled on the country, and a certain sense of relaxation was permitted. The Boer War was over, a new era had started, the British Empire was at its zenith, and the map of the world still showed nearly a quarter of it coloured in British imperial red. The soldiers who had sung 'Good-bye, Dolly, I must leave you' had come back to Dolly, and sporting straw hats they strolled in the parks with their ladyloves, whose long dresses still at this time swept the ground. Peace reigned as they, and we, listened to the German bands, but it was a very deceptive calm, masking hardship, and sometimes destitution. Barnardo's alone, not to mention all the other charitable institutions operating in London in the early years of the century, had thousands of children in its care.

So, from the very beginning you stood on your own two tiny toddler feet, and got on with it. No moaning. The cows got more attention.

These cows – practically members of the family – were kept by my mother. Actually, it would be more appropriate to say they kept us. Brown cows they were. Not Friesland, or Jersey, or any other fancy pedigree cows, but common or garden crossbred cows with names like Tilly and Butter. I was particularly attached to our cow, Tilly. So was my mother, for milk meant money, and Tilly had a high milk yield; she was sometimes the greatest source of revenue coming into our home. Consequently, in my mother's eyes, she was her most valuable possession, and she and her sisters were under constant vigilance. In winter, my mother kept them in the yard behind the house. In summer they grazed in the fields which ran to Grove Vale, the entrance to which was under the arch behind the dairy shop. She had been left the cows and the dairy by her first husband, who had died of a heart attack, and there she was, a widow with five children and no other means of support for herself and her family. So she kept the cows. She mucked out, milked, and ran the shop, which was located diagonally opposite in the archway over the road. The location was only three miles from the heart of London.

She was forty-one at the time. She was independent, fed her children, and somehow made a living. At the turn of the century people did this without a second thought. They were born and bred with backbone. There was no DHSS. If you didn't find a way to survive, you went to the wall. For my mother, it was cows. Indeed, for us all, it was cows. Cows were the difference between eating and starving.

The address where all this struggle went on was No. 1 Adys Road in East Dulwich, and the yard at the back of the house and the archway to the fields and the dairy shop are there to this day. But not the house or the fields, and the dairy shop now belongs to a motor mechanic. The house was a Victorian house, brick built, but not very big, and it had no bathroom or indoor toilet. Into it were crammed all eight of us. But the yard was quite big, and besides the cows, my uncle stabled ten horses and carts there for use in his haulage business.

In 1900 my mother took on a young man to do the milk round, and when her husband died she promptly married the roundsman. He was to become my father. He was twenty-one and my mother was twenty years his senior at the time of their marriage. Not only did he marry her, he also accepted responsibility for her children, the eldest of whom was only ten years younger than he. I was their first and only child, and it was into this ready-made family of children, cows, carts and horses that I was born at the beginning of the century: on 22nd July 1902.

My first recollection of Adys Road was being summoned by an old lady who lived a few doors away, and her asking me to go and buy her a pennyworth of tea from the general shop over the road. I was about three at the time. For doing this errand she gave me a farthing for sweets. However, the attraction of the sweets got the better of me and having bought them, but not the tea, I proceeded home where I was severely chastised, and, the error of my ways having been pointed out to me, I was sent back for the old lady's original purchase.

Soon after this we set out on the first of our several moves. On this occasion it was to Peckham, but my mother didn't like it, and I certainly didn't approve of the new district. I left home. After playing in the street one evening, despite my brother's warning to come indoors at nightfall, I made off and was eventually found on Walworth Road by a policeman who took me to the police station. There I got tea and cake. It was well worth leaving home for! I planned to do it again, for I very much enjoyed not only the free refreshments but all the attention lavished on me, and I was really quite sorry when my mother and father came to fetch me.

We moved house again quite quickly after that, back to Dulwich. But I didn't do much wandering. I was confined to the house. Chickenpox. Mumps. Ringworm. Whatever child's ailment had been invented, I got it. I couldn't go to school. In fact I never got there till I was seven. As for the ringworm, it just wouldn't go. I had to be taken to the old Charing Cross Hospital in the Strand where they shaved all my lovely fair hair off. I was absolutely bald. But it had its compensations. Going for treatment, I also got to go and see the Changing of the Guard which was close by in Whitehall, and on another highly exciting occasion we, my mother and I, even went as far as Buckingham Palace, where my father was painting the railings!

How to keep me amused? My father had the idea of making me a wheelbarrow out of a box and pram wheels. And I put it, I thought, to very good use by going to the greengrocer's and filling it with carrots and potatoes to take home. Oh, the disappointment! My mother wasn't pleased. In fact, she was quite displeased. I was made to take them back. How could they do this to me, especially as old Mr Dring, the greengrocer, knew nothing about his loss, for he hadn't been looking when I took them? I explained this to my mother, but she didn't seem to care. Nor did she appreciate the free coal I brought home for her in my wheelbarrow, also from the same source. Why had they given me this useful toy, when my efforts on their behalf were not appreciated?

But my young life was not exclusively devoted to bringing home the bacon. I had other tasks to attend to. My other self-appointed job in life was to be helpful to the ladies, and I was particularly pleased – frequently, in the case of Jessie Greenwood's knickers – to offer any delicate assistance they might require. Jessie Greenwood's knickers seemed to fall down quite often, and this entailed much kneeling on the ground on my part in order that I might reach the buttons. It was while I was on my hands and knees at this occupation that a neighbour saw me and reported my activities to my mother. More trouble. I truly tried to be the Good Samaritan as instructed in Sunday School. I even gamely tried to please the other children by catching tin cans when they wanted to play ball but didn't have one. Even that caused me pain, as I ended up with a lacerated finger, the scar of which I still have.

It was decided Sunday School was not enough. Church proper must also be prevailed upon to play its part in reforming my character, and teaching me the way I ought to go. Thus, was I duly despatched to Matins, only to be placed behind a lady who removed her white fur muff and tantalisingly placed it on the seat before me. Ah, here was a place where I could still entertain myself. Correction wasn't so bad after all. Silently I plucked the fur and blew it up into the air. Roofwards it floated. The vicar looked. He frowned. He spoke. And out I went. I had been so quiet. How could anyone complain? 'Be seen, and not heard,' they said. And wasn't I doing just that? For I was a helpful little boy. All I wanted was to please. I never could comprehend why my efforts on other people's behalf, such enterprising efforts, too, met with so much displeasure. No one seemed to understand me.

Heber Road – At Last!

It was 1909, and school suddenly interrupted my entrepreneurial activities. I was seven, quite old really, when I, John William Humphrey Gilbert, with short fair hair and short grey trousers, having suffered every illness known to English childhood, finally got enrolled at Heber Road School, grace of the London County Council.

I carried with me my lunch and satchel, plus the determination to be good, to be as quiet as a mouse, so that at last everyone would be proud of me, and with more than a little apprehension I stepped into that child's world of double desks and coloured chalk, of the school piano and the infants' toilets, of dirt, and poverty, and black and white engraved prints that always had a moral. I was seven, and ought not to have been afraid, but I knew the other children had a two year start ahead of me.

My mother took me to the school. And left me at the gate. So that was it. The school, with two huge oblong motifs embedded either side of the main door, stating that the LCC had built it in the late nineteenth century, would every day from now on loom up in front of me, red brick and solid and forbidding. It was the windows that worried me most. They were like great eyes in an ogre head. The important ones were flanked by ochre-coloured decorative panels and the others were decorated with bright red tiles. From the outside they didn't look so bad, but once inside they proved to be windows that no little boy could see out of. They guarded the sweaty ground floor hall where we did physical training, up and down, up and down, up and down, ten times for each exercise, and also the assembly hall where we regularly sang 'All Things Bright and Beautiful', as well as the rooms for the babies, the infants and the juniors.

I fitted in nowhere. At seven, I was far too old to be a baby, who slept for part of each school day on a mat on the hall floor in a row, and even too old to be an infant, who also rested, arms folded, head down on the desk. ("And don't you dare look up!") So I was put into the charge of Mr Ford, and told to 'catch up'. Every day, at school and at home, I had one special mission thrust upon me. To catch up. Not for me the plasticine box or making trains out of match boxes. No playtime either. Just extra work, extra work, extra work.

And after Mr Ford had pronounced me 'caught up' I was put up-
to Form 4. Think of it. I was a junior! But a junior without the kind
Mr Ford. A junior in the clutches of Mr Whiteman, who was strict,
and I thought I would never last at Heber Road School.

But, I did, for no sooner had I 'gone up' and started unimagined
things like 'penmanship', and had coloured all the bits of the British
Empire pink on a home-made map, than I became one of
Mr Whiteman's favourites, and he stopped calling me by my surname,
as the custom was, and started to call me John. And with this great
honour all my intentions to be good and quiet flew out of those very
windows out of which I could not see. I returned to my former self,
carefree and fearless, and sought out what delights Heber Road might
open up before me. I discovered the supreme joy of playtime, and
games, and the after school curricula which we invented for ourselves.

It was all so exciting. Not for us sitting goggle-eyed in front of the
TV. Even the radio hadn't been invented. Think of it! No computer
games to test our skill. But skill we had. With marbles and glass
alleys, and particularly with cherry stones and screws. To play cherry
stones we sat with our backs to the wall and our legs open. We placed
one screw on its head before us, then we challenged the bigger boys to
knock it down with cherry stones. Sometimes three or four of them
tried together, and when it was down, there was a fight as to whom
should have it, this screw. What for? I have often wondered.

School done, we spent hours outside the tobacconist's close by
Dulwich Library, and as soon as a customer came out we pounced on
him for a cigarette card. Roses. Cricketers. Birds. Film Stars. Oh, the
joy of a John Boles card! ("Swap you for a Charlie Chaplin!")

For exercise, when we tumbled out at four, we had hoops, the
boys' made of iron, and the girls' of wood, and spinning tops of all
shapes and sizes. And if you were really well off, that is, if your
parents were, you might get roller skates. Only rich kids, well, rich
by our standards, got roller skates. They got to do stamp collecting,
too, and were allowed fireworks. Fireworks! A string of crackers.
What bliss we could purchase for 3d. They were two inches long and
there were two hundred of them on a string, painted red with a white
wick. If we couldn't afford to buy fireworks we used to fill the end of
a latch key with live matches, put a piece of string on the other end,
drive in a nail, and then bang it against the wall, where it would make
a terrific noise.

Everything was new, thrilling, fascinating, but over all these activities, indeed, over the whole of my childhood, hovered one abiding word – poverty. And no matter how hard we tried, and we tried very hard, it would never go away. It was as if we lived in two huge scales named 'in work' and 'out of work'. Like the figure of Justice over the Old Bailey, my mother held these scales, and more often than not my father sat in the one named 'out'.

So the day I found a purse with five sovereigns in it was an occasion of great rejoicing. But poor as we were, we never stole or kept anything that wasn't ours. Everything we had had to be worked for. So back the sovereigns had to go, to that self-same greengrocer with whose carrots, potatoes and coal I had earlier in life been so free. He gave my father 2/6d as a reward. That day we got a very good dinner.

More often, however, it was a very poor dinner, and the coal remained firmly in the cellar of the greengrocer's shop. Coal was a great problem. We, like of most of our neighbours, did not have a gas-stove on which we could cook. We had a 'kitchener' which was an open grate, with an oven at the side. It provided everything– heat, hot water, the dinner, even heated irons for ironing. But the problem was where to find the 1/8d per sack that the hundredweight of coal cost to get it going. It was a case of scraping it up, from everywhere and everyone, if you wanted to keep warm and eat.

This, of course, was essential. In those days the winters were hard. And there was always snow for Christmas. If father was in work, which wasn't very often, on Christmas Day we would wait with eager anticipation for a bag of sweets and a toy. If times were hard, then we got only an orange and an apple and very, very few sweets. But even if there was nothing else, there was always the snow. That made us happy. But by afternoon there would hang over us the non-appearance of my sisters who were in service, and never allowed to come home then. I can remember it as a great sadness, a great gap in the day; it almost brought life to a stop.

As did the appearance of the insurance man each week for the collection of 1d on the life of each adult in the house, so that he or she could have a decent funeral and burial. These insurance policies lasted twenty-five years, and if you hadn't died by then you got a free policy until you did. If you had no policy you got to be buried in a pauper's grave at the expense of the parish, which everyone feared. It was a disgrace, and always in mind, for death and poverty were always with us, and the insurance man was just one of those who plied their trade in the streets.

Not that they were all so morbid. There was the tally man who sold clothes on the cheap for a few pence each week, depending upon what you could afford, which was usually precious little. He was followed by the windmill man, so called because he gave you a cellophane windmill, and, if you were lucky, a balloon as well, in return for old jam jars. The horse meat man with lumps of meat on a skewer for ½d came followed by several cats. The fish man was even more popular with the cats because when a customer had the head cut off a bloater it was thrown to the cats and a fight always ensued. Then there was the winkle and shrimp man, who only came out on Sundays, as did the crumpet man with his tray on his head, ringing a little bell as he went to let you know he was coming. You could buy eight crumpets for 3d. The milkman came very early and woke us all up before dawn, rattling metal milk cans. Everything was brought to you in the street. You could even have a paper delivered if you could afford it. There was a great choice: *The Daily News, Chronicle, The Mirror, Sketch, Express*, and *Herald* were ½d each; the *Telegraph* was 1d, and *The Times* 2d. Hardly anyone I ever knew took *The Times*. You had to be in a regular job to afford such a luxury.

"Such Larks, Pip"
Great Expectations, Charles Dickens

I knew all about this because quite early on, among other things, I became a paper boy, and my life from that time became divided into two halves – school and work. Both halves had their lighter side; school provided games, which I loved, and work, well, work had the added attraction of larks. And sometimes it seemed to me they were all the same – larks, work, games, school.

So it was that I grew up and moved from one class to another. Each class had forty or so boys in it and was divided into sections with a captain, and each section competed in all subjects and sports. I was a captain, but being captain didn't mean you could miss lessons. Oh, no, not even on sports day. Thus, when my last sports day came and I was scheduled for woodwork, woodwork it had to be. But my friends didn't let me down. They said they would enter me for the events, and they did. They entered me for everything possible. The eighty yard sprint, the relay race, the wheelbarrow race, even the three-legged race. They also put me down for cricket and football. And I won, and won, and won. I couldn't seem to lose. I loved every minute of it.

I was very sorry to leave. And the last six weeks were very memorable to me as it was at the time of the great flu epidemic and many of the teachers were ill, so my friend and I were put in charge of the third form boys. Was I proud! I was a schoolteacher! But it had to end, and the day came for saying goodbye to Mr Whiteman. Well, sad as it was, we went to do it, but he'd already gone, so my friend and I ran all the way to Goose Green before we were able to catch up with him. He was really pleased to see us, so it was worth it.

But someone who was never pleased to see us was the lamplighter who used to come at dusk to turn on the street lights, and sometimes, for fun, we bigger boys would scale the posts and blow out the pilot lights. Then we'd hide, and watch for the lamplighter, who, cursing, and much to our delight, would have to climb up the post to re-light the pilot light before he could continue with his round. And when he did, he'd find we'd extinguished the next one as well. We thought this was a great lark. Looking back on it, it was cruel, in a way, for he was probably not young. We didn't understand that then, but we never indulged in the deliberate cruelty which has become a feature of our times. No boy I knew would have ever hurt an elderly person, a child, or an animal.

I was ten when I went to my first football match, at Crystal Palace. I was taken by my favourite brother, Victor, and from that day on I was a fervent supporter. But to attend every week couldn't be done. We couldn't pay the entrance fee. Instead, we used to content ourselves with watching Townley Park playing by the side of Alleyn's School. It was an art to get to see these matches. The authorities used to put up cover screens all round the pitch so that nobody could see the game. We used to hang around until the doorman wasn't looking and then sneak in. If he spotted us he threw us out. But if he thought we had behaved ourselves he would let us in at half-time, provided that we promised to keep quiet. Other than that, football was restricted to playing by ourselves on Dulwich Common. As I had two paper rounds at the time, the walking to deliver the papers and the playing of football meant the soles of my shoes were always getting very thin. It was a lucky thing for me that my father could mend shoes, otherwise it is true to say I would have been virtually barefooted. As it was, my feet were often wet and cold, especially in snow or slush, and I made up my mind then that when I grew up I would earn enough money always to have good shoes.

Then there was fishing. Fishing, that is, from the private and therefore forbidden duck pond at the corner of Alleyn Road. It is still there, that pond. We used to throw a piece of string over the railings and if we caught a fish we pulled it on to the grass and then, shrieking with triumph, jumped over to retrieve it. We considered this one of our most daring larks; there was always the chance of being caught the wrong side of the railings and getting your ears boxed by the keeper. My father also took me 'proper' fishing in the lake at Red Post Hill. He caught carp. I caught tiddlers. We had string and worms. We also had a tin bath in the garden where we kept the fish we caught, and sometimes we had so many we had to stop fishing for a while.

After a time, of course, I graduated from cherry stones and cigarette cards, and took an interest in more grown-up things such as the cinema, where a lady played the piano all the time and the films were always about Cowboys and Indians. Or I pinched my brothers' papers, *The Magnet* and *The Gem*. I even pinched my brother's fretsaw and got into terrible trouble if I broke the blade, so after a time I went in for outdoor pursuits which seemed to suit me better. I spent a lot of time studying Jim Bacon's pigeons, or helping my uncle with the horses. I liked that, even mucking out.

Horses were a status symbol, and they seemed even more important if you kept them in your own backyard where the cows used to be. It was our answer to the men who lived opposite and who used to drive the new horse buses. They came home very full of themselves with their whips and their blankets over their arms, strutting along as if they owned the street. They were, they considered, in every way superior to us and to our neighbour, Mr Sadler, who drove a coal cart. The Sadlers lodged a gravedigger who was even lower down the social scale. I was always most interested to know if he would be allowed to dig his own grave as a sort of perk, but no one would tell me.

Once while exploring Dulwich Park I found the beautiful garden of a big house called The Elms which had large wooden gates. In the garden were all sorts of fruit trees, including a mulberry tree, and lots of fruit bushes, and as gooseberries were a great favourite of mine I was highly delighted. I told my friends and we climbed the wall and helped ourselves. But when the fruit season was finished, I still went back for it was a beautiful place and I enjoyed going there by myself. I also liked to get into the grounds of Dulwich College for the same reason, not just to obtain conkers, though that was undeniably a big attraction. We used to keep going back to these places, but we always eventually got chased away by a policeman or a keeper.

I told my friends what I had found and got them into the gardens, and they in return told me about their finds. What the Andrews brothers found was the Band of Good Hope. So I went there, too. My father told me I would never be able to have an alcoholic drink when I grew up because, having joined that organisation, I had taken the pledge. He thought it was a great joke, but I was very worried about this future restriction on my adult life, so I switched my allegiance to the Harrington boys instead and went back to the Sunday School where I had been sent as a corrective measure as a very young child. There, after behaving myself for a while, I was allowed to go on the Sunday School outing which turned out to be a day at Bognor and was the first time I had seen the sea. Unfortunately, playing on the struts under the pier, I slipped and got soaked and had to spend the day being dried off by a lavatory attendant in the toilets. So it wasn't such a good idea after all. Nor was the Scouts. I joined that, too, with great enthusiasm, but my mother was furious as the uniform cost 18/- and there was absolutely no way this could be provided.

But I didn't really mind. The Scouts was the Scouts and unproductive.

A paper round was a quite different kind of ball game. It paid. At first I used to go with my brother, then with one of the Harrington boys, and when he gave it up to start real work I was given the job. It was very hard. It meant getting up at 5.30 a.m. to walk the 1½ miles to Wood Vale, doing the paper round which ended at the lodge in Dulwich Park, and then getting home for breakfast by 8.15 a.m. and being at school at 9 a.m. It all had to be done again in the evening, and took from 5 p.m. to 7 p.m. I got 2/6d a week, and I was allowed to keep 2d pocket money.

I felt I was a real businessman. There was a war on. I could, I would do anything. Except... for the one job I hated. It was going to the pawn shop for my mother. You see, every Monday my mother would pawn my brothers' suits in order to buy the week's food; then, when they came home with their wages on Saturday, I would be sent to get the clothes out of pawn so that they could wear them on Sunday. But she never told them that she was doing this, and when they found out there was the most terrible row. As a reward for going to the pawn shop she sometimes bought me a halfpenny egg. It was something special and I wanted it boiled. Whenever my boiled egg was bad I took it back to the grocer, but he invariably said he had not guaranteed that his eggs could be boiled. Eggs, like everything else that was not a bare necessity, were a luxury. So was gas. It crept up upon us, slowly, taking over from the oil lamp and candles. It glowed down upon us out of small white incandescent bulbs, and was never put on until dark.

That's why spring, with its longer days, was so lovely. It was a delight, and the summer lasted and lasted, broken only by the occasional thunderstorm of which we always had forewarning because my mother was terrified of thunder and knew when it was in the air. She used to hide in the summer-empty coal cellar until I told her it had passed. Then autumn seemed to go so quickly, and it was no time at all till the fogs started, regular as clockwork each November, owing to the coal fires that everybody started to light.

We only ever had a real fire on Sunday afternoons in the parlour, so that my father and brothers could rest after their dinner, and before the troubles of the week to come. I used to be sent to the off-licence for a pint of porter for a 1d on tick, but once I'd fetched it for them, it was bed for me, in an icy bedroom. It was so cold that icicles hung on the windows, and the only way to get the bed even a tiny bit warm was to put bricks in the oven, wrap a cloth round them and put them in the bed. I used to long to be like the gentry and own a warming pan, so that our Sunday cinders could be put to good use, and the pan on a long pole moved up and down the bed till it was warm to jump into. This was the second thing that I made up my mind to do; together with getting good shoes, I would get myself a warming pan. I never did, of course, and my bed remained icy cold for many years to come.

But getting in was better than getting out on a damp winter's morning and putting your feet onto cold lino, especially on a Monday. And it wasn't just the cold. The news was bad. People looked grim.

The war was closing in around us. I left my paper round and got a job as an off-licence delivery boy at 3/6d a week, plus a penny here and a penny there in tips. And finally, my uncle, who owned the house, told us to move. So we did. To a bigger one. At last, to our great surprise, and against all the odds, we had more room. It was good in one way, but not in another. Because, for one reason or another, everybody left home.

Chapter Two
The Empty House

The house was big and its address was: 251 Crystal Palace Road. The very name 'Crystal Palace' thrilled me. It conjured up for me not the Crystal Palace of Prince Albert after which it had undoubtedly been named, but a Hans Anderson crystal palace, all turrets and beautiful princesses and knights in shining armour on white chargers. Even to this day, eighty years on, I still miss no opportunity to say it: Crystal Palace. Only now it is usually the football club I am referring to. But I don't mind that. It is the words I relish. It has a lovely sound.

So there we were in a bigger house, and it all seemed very posh to me, and I felt that at last we had put our feet on the first rung of the ladder to becoming part of the elite. A step, I might say, I had no hesitation in considering we truly deserved after so much effort. And imagine! I was no longer going to be a child who had gone to Heber Road School and after school, pressing up against the railings, had watched the Dulwich College boys playing cricket in their whites on their huge pitch with their own castle-like building in the background; I wasn't going to be the mucker-out and groom to someone else's horses, I was going to own them and ride them myself; I wasn't going to be a paper boy, or an off-licence delivery boy, always at some one else's beck and call, counting the pennies and wearing shoes that let the water in. I was going to be the boss.

Furthermore, I was going to be handsome! I would be the prince myself. So, like all boys leaving school, I began to consider how to enhance my appearance. This was, I reasoned, all the more urgent and appropriate, owing to our removal from the proximity of the cow byre and stables to the exalted address in Crystal Palace Road. In my

The Empty House.

case, as I had no funds to do anything whatsoever of a sartorial nature, my efforts took the form of hair cream. But this immediately called forth the remark that if I ran too fast whilst competing in any of my favourite sports it would all run down my face. Added to this there appeared on the scene a young man who, whilst indicating that he wished to become better acquainted with one of my sisters, invariably had his younger brother with him. This boy always wore a velvet suit, and it became a great source of amusement to my family to tease me by commenting on what a pretty boy this Harold was, how good-looking, and how curly his hair was with no cream on it.

But I didn't care. Good-looking or not, velvet suit or not, and curly hair with or without cream, I was going places. I would show them! And, after all, secretly wasn't I the handsome prince?

But for the moment here we were newly installed in this nice big new posh house and disappointment set in almost immediately. For a start, my sisters had already left home and were in service. Although this had been the case in the smaller house, in a big house space and emptiness made it all the more obvious. They both earned about 5/-d each for one month's work, and were allowed only one half-day a week off, plus each alternate Sunday afternoon. It is strange, that the Sunday afternoons that they did not come home, are the ones that I remember most clearly, and the bigger the new house seemed, the worse their absence seemed.

My two elder brothers also left school at this time and were therefore out all day. Tom became a builder's assistant and started work at 6 a.m. and didn't finish till 6 p.m. Brother Albert managed to get a job at Kodak's in Regent Street which was considered very classy; they paid him 5/-d, not a month, but a week! My third brother continued the good work with the paper rounds until he, too, left school and went as a clerk to a shirt manufacturers in the City, also earning 5/-d a week. However, he, unfortunately, lost his first month's money because it – one sovereign – fell through a hole in his trouser pocket as he was walking home. This was a quite dreadful calamity because he had promised to take me to the pictures when he received his first month's pay. But one of my sisters made up for it by treating me herself. We went to a small hall in Lordship Lane. It wasn't really a cinema at all, but it screened Cowboy and Indian films, and a fat lady played the piano all through the performances.

It was about this time that my eldest sister got herself a boyfriend. He was a tram conductor, judged to be a very good position to hold at that time, and so my mother allowed him to be a gentleman visitor when my sister had her afternoon off.

Moving to Crystal Palace Road meant I made new friends, especially with Jim Bacon whom I had already envied as the owner of the pigeons. Now he was a neighbour. We also made friends with the Matthews family, who had a grocer's shop, always a good thing to have dealings with in uncertain times. I made a point of befriending Stan, their son, but otherwise I had to start from scratch in the friendship stakes. Apart from our moving, almost all the boys I had known apart from these moved or drifted away, and eventually there was no one left with whom I used to go fishing in the duck pond or climb into the big garden. But I didn't mind too much, for my sights were set on the future. I was eager to try my luck in the big wide world, and with my brothers out at work from morning to night, and my sisters away in service, I consoled myself that soon I, too, would be out all day.

An important event in all this self-advancement and job hunting was that Tom changed his job from Malpress & Co, a firm nearby, to become builder's assistant with Fryers Ltd at No. 6 Henrietta Street, London, W1. Although we didn't know it at the time, this was to have repercussions on our lives, mine as well as his.

In the meantime, the war was well under way, and my father was still unemployed. So it was no great surprise when he came home one day and said that he had joined Kitchener's Army. My mother was very upset, as, being out of work, it was always in his mind to do this, and she was equally always mindful of his doing it, and constantly telling him not to do so.

The next thing we knew was that my brothers, Tom and Albert, were both called up. Tom joined the First Surrey Rifles, and Albert joined the Royal Army Medical Corps.

Now the house was really empty – except for me and my mother and my brother, Victor. Only such a short time ago there had been eight people in our family. Now there were just three. It was then when I was in my last days at school that my mother became stricken with arthritis. She had terrible pain in both shoulders and could not move. I used to bathe them first with hot and then with cold water to relieve the pain. Although I was on the point of leaving school, this caused trouble with the school board man, dreaded by every parent and child. He came to the house to find out why I was not at certain lessons, but I think he must have felt sorry for us as, after looking very stern, he arranged for me to be allowed to come home each playtime to look after her.

There were no painkillers, the doctor cost 6/8d a visit, and medicine was 2/-d a bottle. She just had to put up with it. My sister could not help as she had married her gentleman caller and moved to Peckham, and in any case her husband was away at the Front and she was left with a tiny baby to look after, while my other sister had got a job at Peake Freans, the biscuit manufacturers in Bermondsey; so she couldn't help either. It was just left to me to do the best I could. The one thing was that we weren't as hard up as we had been. This was ironical, for when the house had been full there were times when we couldn't even buy coal to light the kitchener to cook or keep warm. The reason for our rather better circumstances was that Tom received £1 a week from Fryers and Albert got 10/-d a week returnance money from Kodak's. Then there was also the small amount of army pay which we had on account of my father's army service.

During all this time I played a lot of cricket and football. I was selected to play in the East London and West London Schools match. It was between me and another boy out of the whole of east London as to whom should be chosen as the slow bowler, but as the other boy came from Grove Vale School and as the teacher in charge also came from that school he was naturally put first and I was made the reserve. But everybody said that I should have been selected and I think so, too. After that I played in my last football match against Dulwich Hamlet (who have in recent years produced Andy Gray) and they beat my team 6–0. I also gave up cricket. In my last match I scored 24 runs, and took three wickets, which was the top score on our side. But again my team lost, a state of affairs I wasn't used to. It was an indication of what was happening to my little world.

Everything was changing. The horse buses were disappearing and petrol buses were taking over. Where many horses had recently been stabled in Milo Road a firm called Airless Resilient Wheels Ltd was in residence. But not for long. They in their turn gave way to a munitions factory run by the Margett family. One of my brothers knew the Margett son and so my mother approached them to ask if there was a place for me as soon as I could leave school.

A place was found. I left school on Friday, 17th July 1916 and started work on Monday, 20th July 1916 at 8 a.m. I worked from eight in the morning until 8.30 at night with an hour for lunch for 8/10d a week, and it was extremely hard. But I got used to it. For the first three months I had the task of 'square holes'. These were cast iron caps which fitted into the tops of bomb cases. You had to file the dirt out of the square hole in order for spanners to fit in and screw the cap on to the cases. It was a very, very monotonous thing to have to do all day. When my three months were up, I was moved on to a drilling machine, and later on to a lathe, and that was a bit more interesting. I shall never, never forget my three months working on the dreadful square holes.

And suddenly everything got terribly expensive, especially food. The few months when, for the first time in our lives, we seemed to have rather more money had gone. Soon I had no clothes. I was getting taller and taller. There was nothing for it. I had to wear my brother's clothes. And my mother had to find a job; she became a tea lady.

When she did this, for the very first time in my life there was no one at home at all. Every afternoon when she went to work, the house at 251 Crystal Palace Road was completely empty, an unknown thing before the First World War. Soon, too, brother Victor would be called up and go.

That left just us two, my mother and me, alone in the house, the house that had once seemed to me not far removed from a castle.

The Call to Arms

My father was wounded four times. You would think that was enough to ask of anyone for his country. He had joined up in September 1914 and had trained at Fareham, near Portsmouth, for three months. Then kitted out and ready, a proud rifleman of the 8th Battalion East Surrey Regiment, he went to France.

At home, however empty, life went on. But what had he gone to? What was the Front Line really like, I used to wonder, for soldiers like my father? We learnt soon afterwards: it was dug-outs and barbed wire and army lorries, soon to be succeeded by endless rain and mud, sentry-go and patrols; the shells, the bully beef and mouldy bread, casualties and more rain and deeper mud followed on. The rats came later.

Everywhere, troops and civilians were singing; essentially, to keep their spirits up. The fighting men sang, 'Mademoiselle from Armentières' and it was all a bit of a joke. At home we gave voice to 'The Spaniard that Blighted my Life' – also supposed to be amusing. But you sensed, even if, like me, a schoolboy with no experience, there was nothing much to be amused or joked about. When you heard the exhortation in the last line of 'Pack up your Troubles' to 'Smile, smile, smile!' you pondered on what the smiles were hiding.

All I knew for certain was that after my father had gone 'over there' we lived in a different world. Time passed, slowly. For one thing, I was terribly tired. I found the munitions factory in which I found myself an awful place to be. I was only fourteen. I was bored, I was exhausted, I was cold. All of a sudden I had crossed the threshold into adulthood, and like my father and brothers before me, indeed, like a person advanced into middle age, I looked forward to the relief of Sunday afternoons so that I could have a good rest. Not that Sunday could be entirely given over to relaxation. As food was so short, I started digging up the garden to grow potatoes. These couldn't be obtained in the shops, only artichokes and swedes, which we didn't like very much. In general food was not only expensive, but scarce.

On top of these deprivations, the air raids on London began. A policeman used to ride around the streets blowing a whistle warning the citizenry to take cover, and sometimes it was several hours before he would reappear shouting: "All clear! All clear!" People were very frightened, especially when the guns were fired, and it wasn't long before rumours were flying about that London would soon be in ruins.

One evening, just as I was coming out of the picture palace at Goose Green, suddenly, what seemed to be a long cigar, all lit up and burning, broke into pieces and fell down out of the sky. It was a very dark, clear night; the stars were shining, and all along Lordship Lane people were gazing upwards. This was the zeppelin which fell at Cuffley, north of London, brought down by Captain Robinson. After that there were no more zeppelin raids.

When I got home I found my mother hiding in the coal cellar under the stairs. She couldn't stop trembling, for, terrified as she was of storms and thunder, this sort of thing, and in particular the gunfire, had the same effect upon her. I was able to inform her that the raid was over and that the zeppelin had been shot down. The news of the war didn't help. It was very sad. Lord Kitchener had been drowned with the sinking of the *Hampshire* battle cruiser, and it was also reported that our army had been driven back in France. There was fierce fighting at Arras.

This was the first occasion on which my father was wounded, by shrapnel in the legs and body. He was sent back for treatment to a hospital in Surrey and came home on leave for a fortnight. After that he had to go back, and when he went my brother Victor, who had been called up and who had joined the Royal Horse Artillery, also set forth for France.

It was all so quiet when they had gone that we were very pleased when a school friend of my brother Albert called on us. His name was Alfred Weller, and he was considered too delicate to fight. He was therefore exempted from the army and allowed to make munitions instead. He became my second sister's boyfriend. My mother, I noticed, said nothing about allowing him, or not allowing him, to call. We were glad of his company, and in the short space of time between my elder sister's courting and now, the rules of etiquette had completely disappeared about gentlemen callers. Women's beaux were no longer vetted by their parents.

In fact, the position of women was never the same again. Owing to the great loss of manpower during hostilities, women took up jobs which the men had been accustomed to doing and were in great demand throughout the whole of England. The gentry had to make do with only two or three maids instead of a whole posse of servants, including a butler and gardener. The men had gone to war and women were emancipated. They changed jobs. They came and went as they pleased, not as the mistress decreed. This attitude spread into all relationships and not only did the younger women not wish to be subservient to an employer, they did not wish to obey husbands either. For the first time many of them, with husbands at the Front, had ample opportunity to do as they pleased and go out, and not to remain in the home all day once they were married, as had been the custom.

That is how it came about that my eldest sister used to visit us every Friday, and, leaving her little baby, George, with my mother, used to go off to the cinema with her own sister-in-law. The great attraction was the new Tower Cinema in Rye Lane, where a silent movie serial called *The Exploits of Elaine* was being shown. This was extremely popular and starred Pearl White as Elaine.

Sometimes, as she got bolder and found her freedom quite exhilarating, my sister used to leave Baby George with us in the evening, too, and in next to no time he was no longer the tiny baby my mother used to mind on Friday afternoons. He began to speak, and his favourite expression was: "All dark. All dark.". To accompany these words he liked to be taken to the door so that he could look out into the night.

It was on just such an occasion when my mother had him in her arms that there was the most terrible explosion and she almost dropped him. The explosion was in the munitions factory at Silvertown, and many, many people were killed. It was dreadful and we all thought that at last the Germans had blown up the whole of London. All this time I kept up my friendship with a lad called Stan White, whom I had originally known at Heber Road School. We used to meet at weekends and go walking, or call on other friends we had made. The evening after the Silvertown explosion his mother and sister came to our house to ask if we knew where he was, as he had left home in the morning and had not returned. His mother was terribly distressed about his disappearance, and was distracted until she finally received a letter from him to say that he could not tolerate the guns and had gone to live in Coulsdon where he had found work in a factory. We were all very shocked by this episode, as, although the guns and bombing were awful, and no one was more frightened than my mother, we did not expect anyone to leave, she least of all.

After all, we were always mindful of the fact that it was far worse for the men at the Front, and just then we got news that my poor father was blown up by a bomb. But this time he was not allowed back to Blighty. He was merely sent down the line to the base for treatment and then returned to his unit.

For us, at home, things went from bad to worse. To make ends meet my mother let a room at the top of our house to an old Irishman and his son, Barney. As they were both unemployed, obviously they were not going to be very good tenants, but we never envisaged that they would actually steal our food. We had to lie in wait all night to catch them creeping into our kitchen, and, when we did, we got rid of them. We did not have enough to eat ourselves, but, even so, we used to try and make up parcels to send to the Front Line, where they were existing only on bully beef and biscuits. Sometimes, if troops were on the move, these parcels never reached them. We were allowed to send food every two months, and it had to weigh not more than 7lbs. The authorities need not have worried; 7lbs of victuals was very hard to come by.

While my father was preparing to return to the Front Line, we heard that there was a terrible battle around the Arras district, with several hundred soldiers being killed. It was a great relief to know he was not there at the time, but, believe me, our relief was short lived, for although he missed that particular fierce attack, it was not long before he was wounded again, on Hill 60 at Ypres, hit by a bullet which fractured his hand, finger and arm.

While he was recuperating he was allowed home, and he took me to the Liberal Club in Lordship Lane, where he was a member. During that week there was an outing, which was a brake ride into the country where they held races. My father entered me in the 100 yards race which, to his delight, I won. I think he was very proud of me, and I had a great desire to please him. Afterwards we played billiards with another man and his son, but my father, who was good at billiards, missed several easy shots.

When I asked him later why he had done this, he said that he did not want to win as the other man was out of work and had no money and the loser had to pay for the drinks.

It was things like this that made me realise I was only just getting to know a little about my father. A lot of the time, because he had been unemployed himself, he had seemed a sad man, but when he had had a couple of drinks he was quite different, and would treat everyone. Beer was much stronger in those days, and despite his fear of going back to the Front Line, he soon became quite a happy person. Gone was the depression that went with being unemployed. He was chirpy, even daring. Another time when I was out with him he told me to hold his arm as he didn't want to salute two officers who were approaching. I don't know why he didn't want to salute them, except that in those days when you met an officer in the street you had to stand to attention and salute; otherwise they could report you.

At this time a new war opened up in the Middle East against the Turkish and Arab countries, and the Germans. Both my brothers, Tom and Albert, were drafted there. The fighting in France in 1917 became very fierce, but gradually the allies were able to make the Germans retreat.

In London the bombing not only continued, but gradually intensified. People were being killed and injured, and houses and buildings destroyed, but fortunately for us Dulwich escaped the worst raids. Aeroplanes used to fly very high and drop very small bombs, then quickly disappear, and it was the noise of the guns that was the more frightening. Everybody had to stop indoors because of the shrapnel; it landed on the roofs and roads, and the next morning all the lads would be out looking for it. During the raids the best thing to do was to get under the table and keep your fingers crossed because there were no air raid shelters. I myself, being young and not fully realising the danger, went visiting as usual, and also took to riding my brother's bicycle to stop it going rusty. Well, that was my story!

Early in 1918 my father was back again and in hospital in England. He was becoming more and more debilitated. This was the fourth time he had been hurt. On this occasion, again in a battle at Ypres, he was wounded in the face, and his nose was broken. The pattern was exactly the same, and we knew that as soon as it was possible he would be posted back. At the same time, my brother Tom, who was a sergeant, still serving in the Middle East, was awarded the Military Medal for bravery because he took charge of the battalion when the officers were wounded. My brother Albert, who hated violence, was still with the Medical Corps, and it used to make him physically ill to go out and collect the wounded with the other medical staff. Brother Victor wouldn't fight at all, and was in charge of the mules and horses which pulled the gun carriages. He said the mules were especially stubborn, but having been accustomed to the horses in Adys Road, he could persuade them, when others couldn't. He was not only a friend to the dumb animals, but to all his comrades; they all loved Victor.

It was about this time that I decided I would be confirmed. My mother said that this wasn't possible as I hadn't been christened, so this ceremony was arranged for one evening. Before it my mother became very faint and had to be carried into the nearby public house. But when the confirmation ceremony took place all went well, nobody fainted, and I became a proper member of the Church of England, with the help of the Bishop of Southwark.

At the end of 1917 a strange thing happened. My father came home on leave and took me to Sutton to visit his eldest brother, who, I was informed, lived with his mother. This lady was, of course, my grandmother. But I had never known that I had a grandmother. She was a very old lady when I first met her, and I never saw her again. I would dearly like to know why my father had never mentioned her.

Before the year ended my youngest sister had become very nervous in the air raids, and it was therefore decided that we would all go to some relations at Hoddesden in Hertfordshire for a week's holiday to get away from the guns and the bombs. We went to stay with my uncle who was my mother's brother, and who was a gardener in a very big house. This was the first real holiday I had ever had. I spent it picking apples for storage, and horrifying Uncle Charlie's wife by asking how to tell the difference between a bull and a cow. My question wasn't meant to be facetious. Although I was nearly sixteen, I was very green, had never been to the country before, and I really didn't know. But my aunt definitely did not approve of my question. Nor, I gathered, did she approve of the seventeen public houses that stood in Hoddesden High Street, for she was a strict teetotaller.

When we returned at the beginning of August 1918, my father had two weeks' leave. When it was up we all went with him to Waterloo Station where he was to take the train for embarkation. The station was packed with servicemen. Everyone was required for a last push to drive the Germans out of France. But my father didn't want to go. He kept saying, "If I go again, I shall never come back." Suddenly he threw off all his kit. "I'm not going back there," he shouted. "I've had enough of it!"

I noticed that two officers were looking over at him, and I drew the attention of the rest of the family to the situation, so that we were all able to close round him and persuade him to put the kit back on, which he did. But it all ended in tears on everybody's part, and it was in the greatest despair that he got on the train to go away.

In early September my mother had a telegram from the War Office to say my father had been killed. He had been killed by a sniper, not even in battle. The official wording later recorded "Killed in Action". It was a terrible shock to my mother, who never ceased to grieve. Over and over again she said, "Why did they send him back to the Front? He wasn't fit. He'd served for four years. Why? Why? Why? You would think to be wounded four times was enough to ask of anyone for their country."

I shall never forget that day, I can truthfully say it is one my mother and I never recovered from. Those who direct the fighting, those who plan war in offices, do not receive news, let alone get torn to bits in the blood and mud. And we lived it all again when documents arrived from his Regiment confirming his death, when a bit of paper was sent about his possessions, when his medals came, and finally when we got a letter from Buckingham palace. A letter from the King and Queen acknowledging a debt to a rifleman in the East Surrey Regiment. Did they, did anyone, suffer what we suffered? I think not. We were supposed to be proud of the letter from Buckingham Palace where I had once been taken to see him painting the railings. I wonder what his thoughts would have been had he known that one day a note would be sent from there to his wife regarding his death? He was forty-three, in the prime of life. Apart from the war, he had had a very hard life, and maybe after the war he could have prospered in the years to come, for he wasn't afraid of work. He certainly deserved to prosper. I was just sixteen, and getting to know him. He was kind and helpful to me and everyone. I was greatly looking forward to going out and about with him when things got back to normal. But – as he had predicted – he never came back. On November 11th 1918 we were told at the munitions works that the war had ended, and we were sent home for the rest of the day. A sort of holiday, for winning. But we had nothing to rejoice over.

BUCKINGHAM PALACE.

I join with my grateful people
in sending you this memorial
of a brave life given for others
in the Great War.

George R.I.

IN
EVER LOVING MEMORY
OF

1914 · 1918

WHO GAVE HIS LIFE FOR
ENGLAND
IN THE GREAT WAR
AND
WHOSE NAME IS ENGRAVED
AT
VIS EN ARTOIS MEMORIAL
FRANCE

Condolence from His Majesty George V in memory of the author's father in World War I.

Chapter Three
A Proper Toff in a Land Fit for Heroes

It had been early in September 1918 when, coming home from work, I had found my mother in tears. There on the table lay the telegram from the War Office. My father had been killed.

I did not know what to do. We just sat together, crying.

The shock of my father's death lasted a long time. The news of it lodged in every part of the house. It perched in rooms and cupboards, and in the kitchen, where he would never again sit and eat his bacon sandwich or drink his strong cup of tea. It hung on the air hooked up behind the lace curtains that veiled Crystal Palace Road, and was hiding in the coal cellar when I went to get the evening coal. Like a living presence it crept along the mantelpiece watched by my mother, and came to rest behind the clock. It sat on top of the sentimental Victorian prints framed in the sitting room alcoves, and climbed up the flowers on the wallpaper. Worse still, at night, it waited in the shadows at the top of the landing, and slid down the banisters to meet me as I went up to bed. It lurked in the very air.

I was sixteen. I was supposed to be grown up, someone for my mother to lean on. "She's all right," the others said between themselves, "She's got Jack."

So I couldn't be openly upset. I did my grieving alone down at the bottom of the garden. And in order to leave the garden I joined the Herne Hill Harriers. They were very kind to me and gave me running shoes and shorts, and taught me how to run and distance myself; they let me become part of their club which met in The Greyhound in Dulwich Village; and from there we used to run twice a week during the winter months, often round the beautiful Dulwich Park. That first winter I wished and wished the spring would come, and when it did, so did the daffodils, and I can remember the jolt it gave me when I realised my father would never see them again.

But I didn't stop running. For I ran in order to forget. And by and large I did forget. Till I opened the front gate. Then war, and what it meant for the common man, hit me between the eyes. Every day, and every night, until the next morning, when I left the house to go to work.

I still worked in what had been the munitions factory, though as soon as the war was over the Government naturally cancelled all the contracts for munitions. Luckily, after being slack for a short while, the factory secured a contract to make car parts, and at first there seemed to be quite a lot of work about either doing this sort of thing or in the building trade, because buildings everywhere, on account of war damage or neglect, needed repairing.

It was all right while it lasted, but it didn't last very long, despite all the promises of the Lloyd George Government that the men returning from the Front would have a land fit for heroes to live in. All the fighting men who had jobs to go to were quickly settled, and those who had escaped with their lives but had no job to go to flooded the market. Soon there was no work for the men returning from the Front, and certainly no work for lads like me who hadn't been old enough to be sent to Arras or the Somme. I, and many like me, were put on short time or sacked. I was sacked.

But I wasn't going to be conquered. I went for an interview at a shop in Rye Lane which wanted salesmen to sell carnival goods for dances and parties. I reckoned that as dances were becoming the rage this might be a good line of business, so with the help of my friend, Stan White (who had come back from Coulsdon), I started up on my own. Between us we bought up glasses, cups and saucers, plates, cutlery and tablecloths, and started catering for dances. More was to come. A friend of mine who was a printer found that his business was thriving to such an extent that he had too much work, so he suggested that instead of his printing the invitation cards which were part of my overall catering service, I should do them myself. He fixed me up with a hand printing machine and several kinds of type, and after a great struggle and a lot of patience on my part I was able to print all sorts of dance cards as well as the next man. I purchased all my cards and stationery from John Dickenson's, and altogether I built up quite a nice little business which was earning me £4 a week – much more than I had been earning in the munitions and car parts factory. I even roped in my mother and my sisters to help me, and paid them at the rate of five shillings a function. They did the catering while I carted the cups and saucers, and everything else, to the venues on a barrow. I did everything. And I extended my range of carnival goods to dolls, whenever children were involved, such as a street party or a works' outing. I bought them by the score, and my mother used to sit up all night to dress them. And very pretty they were, too, when she'd finished.

She worked hard. She sewed and she listened. She listened, as I did, for one of Kitchener's Army who would never return. And sometimes she bit her lip and wiped away her tears, and I could see that the doll she was working on had become quite wet. It's at such times that it's hard for a boy trying to take his father's place.

And I got lonely, too, so when the father of a boy who had been a friend of mine at school asked me if I would like a job canvassing for a newspaper I said yes. It would get me out and about.

The paper was *The Daily News*, and I had to go to Brixton Town Hall where the manager of the sales drive was arranging a canvassing party. Behind the idea was an insurance scheme in association with the paper, which cost one penny a day. If you took the paper each day for so many months you would be insured against a broken leg or arm and would receive £2 a week for six weeks. This appealed especially to families who had children, and it was usually the mother who was anxious to take the paper.

We were paid ten shillings a day, and sixpence for every order we were able to get. This was quite a good wage in those days. We used to spend about two weeks in each area and then move on to somewhere new. To begin with we scoured London. This lasted all the summer, but as the autumn approached we were sent further and further afield, starting at such places as Watford and St Albans, and then moving out to Reading, and other towns, like Oxford. As soon as we began working outside London our remuneration went up to fifteen shillings a day, which was a godsend to my mother and me. There was the additional benefit that this sort of work enabled me to move around the country and see places I had never seen before, and also to meet many sorts of people, which was worth more than money, as it gave me confidence.

Of course, it was hard and we often had to board away from home, but the greatest difficulty outside London was trying to sell the paper in Conservative districts. The country areas were, generally speaking, more Conservative than the towns, and as *The Daily News* was a Labour paper, getting orders was virtually impossible. Finally *The Daily News* decided to finish with the insurance scheme, and I was asked to look for other employment.

Luckily for me, my brother Tom had been promised his job back with Fryers, the theatrical decorators, when he returned from the War. He progressed very well there, but Mr de Lissa the owner suddenly decided to dispense with all his men and to sublet all his jobs to outside firms. Thus it was that my brother, and another of Mr de Lissa's employees, a man called Percy Kimber, decided to set up in business on their own, and called their partnership Kimber and James. With Mr de Lissa's help they soon became quite busy, and, to my delight, later on asked me to join them, so I was quickly able to tell *The Daily News* that I would be finishing with them.

My first task was to help decorate a suite of rooms at the Carlton Hotel. It was here I got my first lesson in the harsh world of business, when I, the junior, was left in charge. Not harsh for me, I might add, but for all the men who went out to lunch on Good Friday and weren't back when the boss called in.

"Where are they?" he demanded of me.

"At lunch. At least I think they're at lunch. They were here and they said they were going to lunch," I posited.

"Lunch!" he shouted at me. "It's gone three!"

"Well," I replied, "I don't think they went till rather late."

"Don't give me that," he said. "They had gone to lunch when I came round before. That was one o'clock. Do you know it's gone three?"

He was angry, but not half as angry as he was when they turned up much later very drunk and, needless to say, quite unable to hang wallpaper, or paint. The inevitable followed. They were all dismissed. And I was rapidly promoted, which was a bit of good luck so early in my decorating career, but we all need a bit of luck in life, and this was very much mine.

I didn't like one task, though, which regularly came my way, and which was to take the steps and boards on a barrow to the sites. As the office and yard were situated to the north of Oxford Street, and most of the jobs centred at this time around Grosvenor Square to the south, it was hazardous in the extreme to get these cumbersome pieces of equipment through the London traffic across Oxford Street. I must say I was very relieved when the firm advanced to the point where it was able to hire a van to transport such things, not to mention the gallons of paint I always seemed to be required to deliver. And there was no question of complaining.

Thus it was I grew up. I was learning fast. I worked even harder. I was desperate to succeed – for my mother, if not for myself. I wanted to shine. I wanted to improve myself. I went to evening classes four nights a week. I studied machine drawing and science. I grew more confident. And much, much taller. I discovered that I could hold my own in conversation. And, suddenly, I was ready to spread my wings.

Not, however, till the new me was suitably attired, in a brand new suit. And what a suit! It was a blue suit. My first own suit. I saved up for it week by week, four shillings a time. I felt it was almost too good to put on.

And having got it, a spin-off would undoubtedly be the power to attract the girls. This, however, I soon realised, was going to be almost as difficult as selling *The Daily News* to Conservatives or crossing the Oxford Street traffic with a ladder under my arm. But never mind. Here I was, raring to go, to parade around the bandstand in Horniman's Park, play musical chairs, and wink at the girls. Unfortunately, not many girls winked back, because I couldn't dance. The girls, I noticed, winked at Stan White. He knew the Lancers backwards.

So, I decided that I must, must learn to dance, and to this end I sought out a dancing club. Stan came too, to improve, he said. But I hadn't reckoned with the criticism at home. "Far too forward," said my mother and her relations. But a young man has to do what a young man has to do. If my friends could dance, so must I. So, I pursued to perfection my pressing need to master the foxtrot and the waltz, convinced the girls would fall over themselves to perform with me. But it didn't quite work out like that.

The music in Horniman's Park blared out, the girls looked, and I winked. I was oh, so anxious to try out what I had learned at the dancing club. But the girls weren't so keen. This was, after all, 1920. Nothing happened... and the band played on.

One of Kitchener's Army

In 1921 it played on without me, when my two friends and I decided to go to Ostend, and from there to try and trace where my father was buried. Everyone tried to put me off, saying I was not old enough and that I would be seasick crossing the Channel. In the event, we had a lovely trip on the boat and arrived at the Hotel Boulevard in Ostend without any trouble.

Our pilgrimage was immediately enlivened when, at dinner, the very first evening we shared a table with three Welsh girls. We soon became quite friendly with them, and before the dinner was over had arranged to meet them on the morrow. Things with them looked decidedly more promising than they had with the misses in Horniman's Park, and it wasn't long before we had embarked on an exciting holiday friendship, which couldn't do other than flourish when we attended a race meeting at Breedine where an English horse called 'Tin Tack' was running. We backed it and it won! At fifteen to one! That evening we had a champagne party at the hotel. Just imagine it! Us and champagne – and girls! This, I decided, was life, and not only life, but life as it should be lived.

However, always present in my mind at least, was the real reason for my being there; the purpose of our journey had been to find my father's grave; and so, early one morning, the six of us set off in a hired car across Belgium and France to Albert. From there we continued, soberly now, to Prue Farm about three miles away, where the War Graves' Commission had told me he was buried. This was the actual site of the battle where Allied troops had been killed.

It was impossible to believe that men, my father among them, had been murdered here in this quiet village, where old women in black humped along with bags, always with bags, and little boys, with large brown eyes and dark hair, played in the dust. They played, as I had played around Dulwich Pond, and yet they were different, every one of them dressed in blue and thoughtful, as if the terrible events which had taken place in their village had left an impression upon them, though they had been unborn at the time. Where were their mothers? The street seemed only to contain the old women, surly middle-aged men who wiped the tops of tables outside the *estaminets* so beloved of the British Tommy, and these little boys.

We eventually arrived at the War Graves' cemetery and the Menin Gate Memorial where my father's name was inscribed, but he was not buried there. It turned out that he, with five other comrades, was buried in the churchyard of the village church and each grave was marked with a wooden cross bearing the words "Unknown British Soldier". We were told that in a bombardment, after they had been buried, all six crosses had been destroyed, so no one knew which was which.

All at once our holiday seemed to have finished, and after the very long journey back to the hotel in Ostend, all we could do was to go to bed. Standing alone the next morning looking out to sea I felt as my father must have felt, when he was separated from England and all that it held for him. I understood that this was the real reason for my visit; here was the source of the news that had pervaded our house in Crystal Palace Road, and it was as if by coming here I had created a permanent link with it, almost tangible in its force.

We came back to Dover, and saw the white cliffs. Our heads were full of the Tommies' marching songs, and we hummed 'Pack up your Troubles' and sang 'It's a Long Way to Tickle Mary'. When we thought about it we couldn't believe we had actually seen latter day Mesdemoiselles from Armentières in the flesh. We had sat outside a café drinking Vermouth. We, too, had crossed the Channel. We had been in touch with terror. It had deprived me of a father, and it was a terrible realisation.

The coach driver fell asleep at the wheel on the way back, but no one was hurt. We said good-bye to the Welsh girls, and decided we had had a good time – except... Except what? A shadow had fallen over everything. I knew it could all be traced back to industrialisation and the demand for food, and to that ever present force underlying the balance of power in Europe – the urge to expand, which manifests itself in dynastic rivalries and blatant nationalism. This is what causes politicians and statesmen, universally recognised as having the right to act on behalf of their people, to go to war. It is they who pledge unquestioning men to give their lives in what they are pleased to call a just war. But they themselves, locked in Whitehall, the Dominion Parliaments, the Élysée Palace, or safe in the Capitol, in the USA, committing conscripts to foreign battles, they do not suffer; it is the little people who are sacrificed. What more can I say? Except that, in a way, I, who had never been to war, was also part of Kitchener's Army, and from then on I had come of age.

Home, Sweet Home

It took me some time to settle down when I got back. I couldn't help it. I tried to put it all behind me; I ran whist drives in much the same way as I had run catering facilities. I even immersed myself in the current craze of wireless fever. But the end of the day would still find me pondering on matters that I was ill educated to ponder on.

But the one thing I knew was that home was much more precious. I was ever mindful of the fact that my father had fought in a foreign country for us, for my brothers and sisters, my mother and me.

And then I met Lilian. Lilian was a lady's maid. She was fair, she came from Cornwall, and she worked for Mrs Mills of Wilton Street. I can see her now in my mind's eye, tripping up and down the stairs in her black dress with a white frilly apron and a white cap trimmed with lace. Lilian was quite a girl. And while Mrs Mills was contemplating the new ivory coloured walls in her drawing room, I was engaging Lilian in conversation below stairs. Mrs Mills had such a lot of work done both internally, and externally, and I was there so often, that eventually Mrs Mills' maid put all the girls in Horniman's Park, and the three Welsh girls, out of my head, and I resolved to ask her out.

Lilian

We went to the pictures, to the music hall, to dances, to hear the band, but particularly to the music hall which was then at the climax of its art. For it was an art; many people have said so including Winston Churchill, when Mrs Ormiston Chant and others got the Empire, Leicester Square closed. The performers were always at war with the Theatres and Music Halls Committee of the London County Council which made the theatre managers responsible for the material used on stage, and which was likely to refuse licences to those places of entertainment which permitted saucy songs. Of course, most of the songs were saucy but never explicit, so that the words could get past the committee. But saucy songs they were, and Lilian and I enjoyed them greatly. For one thing, at the music hall we could unwind, and for another they were never *that* bad. And, let me tell you, Lilian herself looked quite saucy, and not a bit like Mrs Mills' maid once she got out of Wilton Street, for she cut a very pretty figure.

So did some of the artistes we went to see. In my time I have seen them all. Earlier, with Stan White, I saw Vesta Tilley, Nellie Wallace, George Robey, Harry Tate, Harry Lauder, and the wonderful Marie Lloyd. Marie Lloyd was a legend in her own lifetime. She was renowned for her generosity to the poor of the East End, which is where she had come from. Her roots were in Bethnal Green and Hoxton, and she first appeared at the Eagle in the City Road. She knew all about poverty and everyone knew about Marie. She could hold an audience in the palm of her hand. She was a true star. And while she was cheering up the working class, privately her life was terribly sad: two of her three husbands beat her up, and when she lived at Oakdene in Golders Green the police from Golders Green or Hendon used to be called to protect her. She was only fifty-two when she died, and I can see her now: enormous blue eyes, bright red lips, fair hair, a plump little figure in a rose coloured dress, all lace and frills and flounces, and above all, her famous wink. It was a national shock when she died, and fifty thousand people lined the route at her funeral.

The time of her death marked the beginning of the downward path of the music hall, but Lilian and I weren't too bothered about that. When entertainment imperceptibly altered to revue and variety we went with it, and in this new form saw the show everybody else saw – *Mr Tower of London*, starring Gracie Fields. We all loved 'Our Gracie'. On the occasion I saw her at the Holborn Empire she told us

Marie Lloyd and her saucy songs of which the following was one:
I always hold in having it if you fancy it
If you fancy it, that's understood
And suppose it makes you fat
I don't worry over that
Cos a little of what you fancy does you good.

that we were to imagine it was the front room and we were having ham and lettuce for tea, ready for a bit of a sing-song. As well as being an actress, a comedienne, and a recording artist, she was a great music hall performer, was Gracie, and like Marie had trouble with husbands, though not with her last, Boris.

As customers to see any of the top-of-the-bill people you had to wait, and a long wait it was. First you had to get a ticket from the man behind the little grill at the bottom of the stone stairs that led up to the upper circle. Then after you'd got in you spent the first few minutes revelling in the atmosphere and studying the red stage curtains, the building's ornate mouldings and cornices, the red wallpaper, and the red plush seats occupied by the well off down below in the stalls. After that you examined the bulging boxes and the little square frames on either side of the stage which would come up in white lights with the numbers of the turns. When the show was about to start the orchestra would come in, and the leader would be visible, but not the players, once they got settled down in the pit for the overture. The show would start with a couple of dancers, followed by a comic or maybe a pianist, a magician or an acrobat, and a tenor would almost certainly close the first half. And all the time the anticipation was mounting, for everyone had really come to see the star and now we hadn't got to wait much longer. The interval was upon us. After what seemed an eternity the orchestra would come back, the little lights on the side of the stage would flick to the last number on the programme, the music would strike up, the curtains part and there she was, if it was Gracie, singing 'Sally, Sally Pride of our Alley', and the applause filled the auditorium.

I have been in many music hall theatres – the Camberwell Palace, the Brixton Empire and the Holborn Empire among them. They have all of them gone, destroyed by enemy action, or pulled down to make way for roads, or houses, or offices. It's the fate of music halls the length and breadth of the land, which is a pity, for they reflected a particular era; they were a bit of social history concerning the working class at the turn of the century; and some of them were beautiful buildings designed by such people as Frank Matcham or W.G.R. Sprague. Sad but there you are, and particularly sad for me that the Holborn Empire should have been destroyed during the Second World War because, apart from seeing Max Miller there, who always

Holborn Empire Programme.

addressed himself to the ladies in the audience and made out the management were listening to see if his jokes would pass the Theatres and Music Halls Committee, it was the venue which featured the big bands which I greatly admired. Jack Hylton, with his vocalists Sam Browne and Dolly Elsie, was my number one favourite, followed by Joe Loss, Jack Payne and Stanley Black.

Well, they've all gone now, including the dear old Flanagan and Allen with the rest of the Crazy Gang who occupied the Victoria Palace. They all lived at Brighton, and after the show, so I'm told, they caught the last train home and played cards all the way. They still make me smile, though it's true to say my taste has changed since then; today I prefer to listen to Pavarotti singing *O, Sole Mio,* or something like that. And it's also true that whenever I think about the old variety theatres, in my imagination it's my father that I see. Somehow, because the music hall was linked with the early days after his death, that is how I remember it, and, of course, Lilian shared that with me.

I was very proud of Lilian, but prouder by far of my father, who actually never went with me to a music hall in his life. Nevertheless, his spirit was always waiting for me when I got back home to Crystal Palace Road after saying goodbye to Lilian. It always came as a jolt, that this was the home he'd gone away to fight for.

Chapter Four
Getting Up to Tricks

Between the wars painting and decorating was not a do-it-yourself affair. Oh, dear me, no! Painters, in particular, suffered a lot, first of all being liable to painters' colic, and secondly by working in a medium that was difficult to handle. In those days, remember, there were no quick drying agents or things like that. You painted, and then waited for it to dry, and sometimes it rained, so you could wait a long time and not get any money because you couldn't finish the job.

It seems odd to think of it now, but at that time paint ruled our lives, for if the paint let us down, our livelihood failed. So, the moment anything was reported amiss with regard to the paint I rushed round to the site, and if I agreed that something was wrong I immediately telephoned the supplier. On one occasion when this happened, The White Paint Company, having checked our consignment and agreed it was not up to standard, brought the whole of their paint production line to a halt. It was discovered that there was a fault on one of their machines, and they were so grateful to us for alerting them to it that, thereafter, for every 500 gallons of paint we bought we got a discount, and they asked us, as a favour, to let them visit special jobs where their paint was being used. But discounts and favours aside, nothing was worth having to scrap work already done.

Then there was the complication of mixing colours. Initially this usually fell to the boss, but once the specification was worked out, the foreman became responsible for producing the correct colour on the site and supplying it to the men carrying out the work. Today, Johnstone's put out over one thousand shades, and no doubt so do ICI and Crown and all the other paint manufacturers. But in my day we only had black and white, the three primaries, red, yellow and blue, and basic brown, green and grey. From these, with staining, you had to make every other colour, and texture, that the client dreamed up.

When I became Percy Kimber's right hand man at the beginning of my career, I used to watch him and then assist him in mixing paint, and after a time I had *my own box* made up. This contained twenty-four colours and white, specially put together by Thomas Parsons and Sons of Oxford Street, and from it, with patience and experimenting, I was soon able to mix any colour. I worked to clients' requests, often with them present, and produced tints for their approval on pieces of board to match curtains and carpets.

In this respect I have to pay tribute here to Percy Kimber. It was he who taught me how to do this, what went with what, and how to obtain such and such a result. Likewise, I must also record my gratitude to Mr Arthur de Lissa, the Chairman of Fryers, who had been my brother's original employer, and who when my brother set up on his own, employed our company. Mr de Lissa, whom I shall mention again in this book, was very generous with his knowledge, provided he felt you were serious and paying attention to him. It was he who taught me that, when arranging a colour scheme for a property, you must always start with the drawing room. This should be in scumbled green or ivory; (and you must try to persuade the client the advantage of this, because in Mr de Lissa's view clients were unbelievably stupid where decorative schemes were concerned.) The dining room should be pine grained, and the study or main room should be walnut grained. The bedroom should always, but always, be tinted in pink. And the second bedroom and main quarters should be papered in a floral design.

Thus it was I learnt not only how to mix colours, but also how to grain and scumble, which were at the time the most popular forms of decoration, and were skills that had to be learnt the hard way – with practice. The grainer had to apply the right colour mix for whatever wood he was imitating – walnut, for example, was a very different shade from pine – and also had to know what sort of pattern pine made, or walnut, or oak, or mahogany, or rosewood, or any other timber the client fancied. Scumbling was slightly easier as it was achieved with one coat of primer, one undercoat, and one top coat, followed by stainings of the required colour rubbed on the walls. It sometimes took as many as four stainings, and there were difficulties when you had to work within a moulding, which was very fashionable. The practice was for the stain to be shaded darker as you got closer to the wood, and then go off light again the other side of it.

How to do it was one of the tricks of the trade, so obviously painters and grainers who were able to mix colours, grain and scumble were in demand. Highly skilled ones such as Mr de Lissa insisted on having were almost impossible to find. To say, even in a time of high unemployment, that they were at a premium is an understatement. But sometimes results were out of the hands of craftsmen, no matter how skilled. And so it was when Mrs Hanbury of Hanbury, Truman and Buxton, a valued client introduced to us by Peter Jones, took exception to the tint on the wall in her boardroom, and I was, to say the least of it, apprehensive, for Mrs Hanbury was the Chairman and Queen Bee of Truman's Brewery in Brick Lane.

Actually, I was anxious right from the start, for when we arrived on site at the brewery the management said the men could visit the still room and help themselves to free beer from the barrels that stood on the side walls. I was appalled and very concerned lest they should take advantage of this, indulge too much, and all be drunk by midday and unable to paint.

This did not happen. But what did happen was that Mrs Hanbury and her directors said they did not like the new colour at all. At first I could not understand why, as pattern boards had been approved for all the various rooms, and in particular for the large boardroom, which was an elegant room that housed all the portraits of the founders and various directors, and in here a sample wall had been painted in a stippled green tint, exactly as required.

Mrs Hanbury, whom I remember as a most dominant, well proportioned lady, with a loud voice, and her directors came to give the wall their approval on a fine summer's day with bright sunshine, and this caused the colour of the red brick wall outside to reflect a pink tint on to our newly painted wall of stippled green.

Mrs Hanbury and her directors did not like it one little bit, and asked me to alter it, saying they would come back the next afternoon. When they had departed, I told my foreman not to touch it as I was sure the colour was right and that the sunlight was causing the fault. This turned out to be correct, and the next day, there being no sun, when Mrs Hanbury and her directors came to view the sample they approved the colour.

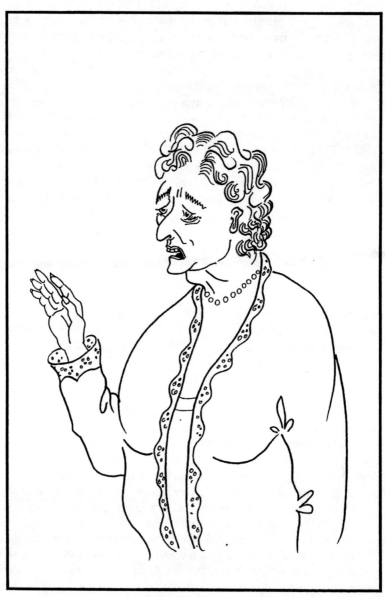

Mrs Hanbury.

"Ah, that is much better," beamed Mrs Hanbury, quite unaware that it was the light that had changed and not the tint on the wall.

And sometimes it wasn't even people who were difficult to manage, it was the equipment, and this was so with a piece of equipment that we called 'The Big Stick'.

In the early days there were no extension ladders and tubular scaffolding had not come into existence. So when we had a contract to paint the outside of large, tall houses such as those in Montague Square or Bryanston Square, where the houses consisted of a basement and four or five storeys reaching to sixty or seventy feet high, we had to hire a large wooden ladder of about seventy or eighty rungs from Stephens & Carter in Harrow Road, and this we called 'The Big Stick'. It enabled us to reach the top windows and large overhanging plaster cornices at the top of the building. The ladder was brought to us on a horse drawn cart at about seven o'clock in the morning in order to avoid the traffic. It took seven men to erect the ladder from the pavement to the top of the building, and was a work of art to accomplish. We used to have three men at the foot of the ladder, and four men in a top floor window, usually a maid's bedroom. A long, heavy rope was tied about ten rungs from the top of the ladder, and when ready the three men at the foot pushed and the four men at the top pulled until the ladder was raised up into position. Sometimes it could happen that the ladder got caught underneath the protruding cornice, and it would take a long while to get it over the top. When it was finally in position, a heavy weight was placed in the gutter and tied to the ladder to stop it from moving.

It was a heart-stopping operation for all concerned, but we all knew it had to be done if the work was to be carried out.

The Silver Lining

I have usually found that, although happiness is not a quality to be banked on, most clouds do have their silver lining. The black cloud beginning to move over England at this time was the threat of a General Strike. It seemed, or rather it seemed to me, that the First World War was no sooner over than rumblings of the General Strike began. Indeed, looking back now, to me the First World War, the General Strike and the Second World War, seem almost continuous.

But with a difference. War, when it comes, appears to be a sudden calamity. Of course, the reasons leading up to it may go back many, even hundreds, of years, but to the population at large it is something that descends upon the country out of the blue. In contrast, the General Strike was in the air, threatening everyone, for a long, long time. It loomed over us, and had us all worried, for everyone was going to be affected.

War is somehow different in its effect. The nation is stirred by its national memory, its shared past (something politicians seem gravely unaware of today, if I may say so), and it girds itself psychologically and physically for the onslaught. But the General Strike was dreadful in so far as some of us were actively striving to keep the country going; and some were static. We were divided in a way that is worse than war – brother against brother. And in a sense, in 1926, we were all stunned.

We had, therefore, to find a way to cope and survive. And our silver lining, our great escape route out of the all-pervading atmosphere of gloom this state of affairs engendered was, at this particular moment, the cinema. More even than sport, for in sport you have to move yourself, participate. But in the flicks, for the price of a few pence we were sold dreams, while we remained passively receptive in our cinema seat; passively because we had no idea how to combat this latest national disaster.

So, we used to stand outside the ABC, the Gaumont (the 'Gormon' as it was pronounced by some of its patrons), the Odeon, the Biograph or the Troxy, and there, marshalled by a uniformed commissionaire who was greatly enjoying his little brief authority, we would meekly wait for him to receive a communiqué from inside, telling him how many of us to let in.

"One in the ninepennies, one only, in the ninepennies. Don't all rush. One only. Two singles in the circle. One and six each," he would shout, unsmilingly, for he felt himself to be very important, and if more than the required number moved forward out would come his arm to bar their way.

"Keep close to the wall, please. Move up! Another two singles in the circle."

As he held open the foyer door, a couple who had previously anguished over whether to be split up, when part of the allure was to be together and hold hands, or perhaps two entirely unacquainted individuals, would spring from the head of the queue and gain admittance to wonderland, that expanse of carpet in the middle of which two cashiers sat in a glass box.

Oh, the Astoria! The Astoria, Finsbury Park! How could they knock it down? It had fish swimming in the foyer pool: decorative, gold and silver fish, serving no purpose, when everybody knew that fish were for eating. Cod at sixpence a pound, and here we had useless fish! Then inside the auditorium, when the lights went down, stars appeared in a dark blue ceiling. We all craned our necks to watch them go out. And this was even before the film started.

My lady friend, Lilian, my escapee from one of the West End's big private houses, and I (who declined to be separated by the doorman) allowed this fantasy world to engulf us. We simply enjoyed it, unaware of the machinations of Hollywood. Tinsel Town they called it, but backers, and moguls, dictator directors sucking enormous cigars, the savage jostling for parts, and the antics of Hollywood wives didn't touch us. Tinsel Town was what it was, and like a lit-up tinselled tree at Christmas for lucky children, it came unquestioned into our lives, a refuge from Kimber and James and being at the beck and call of Mrs Mills of Wilson Street. You could almost say that, adults though we were, we, like children, were innocent as we watched, for we neither knew nor cared what made Hollywood tick.

But oh, those celluloid stars! They inhabited that other world of make-believe, where for one and sixpence we, too, could be a Vanderbilt! Or Tom Mix, or Jackie Coogan, or Douglas Fairbanks. (I rather fancied myself as Douglas Fairbanks. I did look a bit like him, I thought, though the accent was difficult to keep up). Or Laura la Plante, or Anna May Wong, or Mary Pickford. I'm sure Lilian was all of these in her dreams, and when we'd finished dreaming, we could both laugh at Charlie Chaplin, Will Hay and Buster Keaton.

I could have fallen in love with Lilian, except that she came from Cornwall, and it seemed a long way to go and see her if she should leave Mrs Mills. But, more importantly, what really stopped me, you see, was that I was already in love with Nova Pilbeam. And who could equal that?

The movie stars were really unique, and they took our breath away. Think of Al Jolson or Irene Dunne! We were awe-struck with wonder, and seduced by their glamour. Above all, they came at an opportune moment, since give or take a few years, they came with the General Strike. And while we watched them, we blocked out, quite deliberately, what it was like to live in England in the Twenties.

Life, with its dreams and its realities, I came to the conclusion, was a very, very difficult affair.

Painter-Improver, That's Me!

One of the worst aspects of the period I am talking about as far as we in business, and struggling to keep in business, were concerned, was the attitude of the clients. This was subtle, for on the one hand they were very glad, at a time when most people were refusing to work, to be able to find firms to carry out their requirements, but on the other hand, they took it out on the men actually doing the job. I, unfortunately, encountered both categories.

One of our contacts at the time was Major Hartigan, who got us the job of redecorating all the rooms in the Grosvenor Hotel, about a hundred of them. When I turned up to discuss the work with him, he immediately started laying down rules, but as it was a very big account there was no question of refusing it.

"Now, my man, I want you to understand this," he began. "It's my paint you'll use when you get under way. Understand? I don't want any paint you buy in. I'm a shareholder in Hatfield's paint, so I want my paint. Now, is that understood before we go any further?"

With my brother and his partner at my back, and men desperate to take home a few shillings to their wives, I could only answer: "Yes, of course, Major Hartigan. I'll see to it."

He nodded in satisfied agreement. On his face, as on Mrs Hanbury's, were the clearly written words, "You just tell these chaps what you want. No messing about. You'll find they knuckle-down. Well, they do for me. But then I'm used to being obeyed."

During this period we came across many like him, including Sir John Jarvis, the builder, Mr de Lissa, who could also be very sharp, and last, but not least, Sir Crispin English who was an orthopaedic surgeon.

Sir Crispin English lived at 86 Brook Street in the West End, and was quite exceptionally strict with the men. No workman was allowed to smoke on his premises. You were hardly allowed to breathe, and if he saw anyone breaking his rules he would order them out of the house and off the job.

On one occasion when we were installing a marble fireplace in his drawing room, he came in and saw the marble mason smoking.

"I do not allow smoking in my house, so you will have to leave at once," he said, and thus ordered out a marble mason who was irreplaceable. When you think of marble masons you think of mass produced funerary memorials, but for some specifications it would be better to think of Michelangelo. A marble mason is often required to be more than a craftsman; he is required to be an artist. That is what Sir Crispin wanted, and that is what Kimber and James supplied him with. Unfortunately, you cannot treat men who consider themselves to be artists, the same as you can get away with treating run-of-the-mill workmen. This particular marble mason went following Sir Crispin's, "No, I won't have you in my house. You must go. It will teach you a lesson. My rules are to be obeyed, that's what I make them for. So, you will have to go. What's more, it will teach the rest of the men."

But, unfortunately for Sir Crispin, and us, the marble mason went, couldn't be replaced, and refused to come back.

Sir Crispin's new fireplace was left unfinished for a very long time.

Of course, there was a funny side to the job, and this revealed itself in the early days of sanitation and drainage, when WC's were first being installed inside the house rather than in the yard or garden. The fitments were placed in the smallest room in the house and were connected to the drainage system with pipes. As at that time water had only just been introduced into houses, a bucket of water was left beside the WC to flush out the pan as required. At first the WC pans were made of porcelain, and fitted with a wooden seat on top, but as time went on the pans became more and more decorative, and in some cases portraits of women were painted in blue on the outside and sometimes even on the inside, too.

Following on from this stage in indoor sanitation, a Mr S. Crapper, who had a shop in the King's Road, Chelsea, invented the water waste preventer, which was referred to as WWP. This consisted of a small tank which was fitted inside with a ball valve and metal arm and shut off valve to stop the water entering the tank beyond a certain level. The tank itself was fitted about seven or eight feet above the WC with a connecting pipe between the two, and finally a chain was affixed to the tank so that the water it held could be released into the pan as required.

In my early days, when this invention first appeared, I was working in a flat in Mortimer Street, W1, on a contract for Fryers Ltd, and the client was a young man of about twenty-five who was about to get married. He visited the flat one day and saw the toilet which was highly decorated in blue with women both inside and outside the pan. He looked alarmed and said to me:

"Is the foreman here?"

I went to get him, and when I presented him the young man announced:

"I can't sit on that – with those women looking at me. What can you do?"

The foreman looked embarrassed, the decorated pan was removed and a plain white porcelain one installed in its place, and Mr de Lissa came along and ordered a commode chair to be made to fit over the pan, as well as a fitting placed over the WWP at ceiling height to close in the tank and the noise. The result was that when the door of the smallest room in this young man's flat was opened, all that could be seen was an armchair and a cupboard joined together with a pipe, which the men thought was quite amusing.

There was also the time I was called to a house in Elvaston Place where a dreadful smell was upsetting the occupants. I went round and round the premises, stalking the smell, being my own Sherlock Holmes, only using my nose instead of my eyes. And then, suddenly, I found *it*. Behind the radiator. *Dead mice*. Mrs Foster, the occupier, was quite a nice lady and terribly grateful to me for getting rid of *their smell*.

Edgar Wallace was quite nice, too, in a quiet sort of way. I called upon him at 20 Portland Place where he wanted his drawing room scumbled in antique ivory. He was a big, thick, plump man, and the longer he was with you the bigger he seemed to grow. It was like *Alice in Wonderland*. You stood there looking at the walls, and he got bigger and bigger, until he seemed enormous and gave you the feeling that his body took up the entire space of the room.

I was not the only one to have this sensation. After we got started, he would come into the drawing room two or three times a day to see how things were progressing. He was always in his dressing gown and smoking a cigarette in a long holder with one hand and carrying a cup of very weak tea in the other. These visits, during which he never spoke, were breaks he made to rest whilst he was dictating his current book to his secretary.

"He gets bigger every time he comes in," one of the men said. "Makes me feel quite peculiar."

And it was true, by the end of the day, when he would remain for the longest period, he had the effect of flattening you against the wall.

I have read that he was renowned for working at a book in the morning, finishing it, and then being at the races in the afternoon. That may be so, but it didn't happen while we were working for him; he worked all day, every day; and although I can't say we exactly looked forward to the moment when the door would open and he would appear, it was, if nothing else, peaceful with him, for he never spoke. Strangely enough, you felt quite safe, even if murder plots were going on in his head.

By the end of 1927 things were getting back to normal, and Kimber and James started to expand again. They landed a big contract with Peter Jones of Sloane Square and once they had this they could consider themselves a big firm.

The jobs that came in from this source were mostly very interesting. We worked on Normanhurst in Hampstead, which was owned by Mr Konstams, whose daughter married Bunny Austin, the tennis champion. But more exciting than Normanhurst for the author, was being sent to Miss Edith Day's who was the big star of *Maid of the Mountains* at Drury Lane. If she had come and inspected the work two or three times a day we would have been delighted; alas, she never came near us! We lived in hope, and left in disappointment.

It was about this time we were asked by Peter Jones to send a carpenter to a house on the Embankment Gardens for work required by Lord Stansgate. After a few days I called to see how my carpenter was getting on as he was nearly finished. He came up to me very worried saying Lord Stansgate had asked him to stay behind and fix up several ornaments, pictures, mirrors etc. which he had brought home from India.

I afterwards said to Lord Stansgate, "I am sorry, sir, but our carpenter cannot do this for you it will have to be done through the firm during working hours."

"Why?" he said, "This has nothing to do with you or the firm."

The next day, our carpenter having finished the work he was asked to do, I took him away.

I cannot say that this episode ended peacefully for I am not easily deterred or put off; and I am still the same today, when I truly believe I'm in the right about something.

Chapter Five

Millie

About this time, my friend, Stan White, who was with the *Daily Mirror,* invited me to their annual dinner and dance at the Café Royale because Jack Hilton's band was in attendance and this was my favourite band at the time. We were all dressed up in our dinner jackets for this occasion.

At the table was a young lady who worked in Stan's office, and she had brought along her cousin Millicent Read. I was at once attracted to Millie, who was a beautiful young lady dressed all in blue. She was quickly introduced to me, and I was extremely happy to meet her, especially since Lilian had gone back to Cornwall and our association had ended.

Millie and I had several dances together and thoroughly enjoyed our evening. In our conversation we found that we had both lived in Dulwich in the same road. I eventually asked for Millie's address, which was the Old Street Police Station, and was told that her father was the Police Superintendent there, in charge of about one hundred men. This information made me somewhat nervous, but not for long. I soon wrote to Millie for an appointment to see her again.

Our first meeting was one evening in Regent Street where we went to the Picture Palace and saw Douglas Fairbanks in *The Iron Mask.* I shall never forget that evening. Millie told me that she worked at United Dairies in Coptic Street, Holborn, where she was head bookkeeper in charge of eight girls. After that, I arranged to meet her every Wednesday evening when we would go to the pictures or a theatre. On Saturday evenings I would call for her about five o'clock when she left her office and we would go to Lyons' Corner House for supper. And on Sundays we always went for a bus ride to Hampton Court, where we had tea and a walk round the gardens, which was most enjoyable.

After about six months' courtship, I went to Old Street to meet Millie's parents. Her mother was a very kind person and we soon became friends. Mr Read, her father, was a big man, six foot two inches tall, weighing some sixteen stone, very upright, loquacious, as well as stern-looking, which he might well be, seeing that he was in charge of a police station in a very tough district, not to mention being in authority over his hundred men. Hindenberg they called him. I also met Tom, Millie's younger brother, who was still at college, and who has been my friend ever since, often spending a day with me at Lord's.

While Millie and I were courting, Mrs Read became ill, and the doctor advised Mr Read to retire and live somewhere quieter. Carrying out doctor's orders they bought 48 Ridgeview Road, Whetstone and, to complete her recovery, before moving Mr Read took his wife away to Weymouth.

Thus it was that while they were in Weymouth Millie and I went to their new house each evening in order to prepare it for their return, and after they had got back and settled down I decided that it was now time for me to act. I formally asked Mr and Mrs Read for the hand of their daughter, which they readily agreed to, and Millie and I went to the jeweller's and selected a diamond ring of her choosing.

About this time, through the office, I was introduced to the Darwin family. They had a house on the Isle of Wight called Brandon House, where Charles Darwin used to live and it was still owned by his descendants. Pattern boards and estimates were prepared and accepted by the family and an order given to start work. The whole of the interior of the house was to be decorated, and it fell to me to take the painters and the foreman there and show them what to do – leaving my new fiancée! I soon got back to London but each week thereafter I had to spend one day on the Isle of Wight inspecting and supervising the work. Every Thursday I left home at six o'clock in the morning, travelled to Waterloo station, and from there to Portsmouth where I took the ferry to Ryde and a taxi to Brandon House four miles away. I usually spent about two hours on the site, and then returned home, arriving about 10.30 p.m. I did this every week until the work was finished.

By now Millie and I were definitely thinking of the future, which meant finding a house to live in and starting to save up to buy furniture. We looked around many places, but were not pleased with the houses we inspected until suddenly we came across a new estate which was just being developed, called Woodside Park. It was ideal as Millie wanted somewhere not far from her parents, and we were so impressed with the houses and the surrounding district that we put our name down for a house in Chanctonbury Way and decided to get married there and then.

After that everything went well, and we were married on the 30th November 1932 at St John's Church in Whetstone.

There was only one cloud on my new horizon: it was that when I moved out of Crystal Palace Road my mother would feel very lonely. After being together all my life, having been brought up by her alone during the First World War, and being alone with her again as one by one my brothers and sisters had left to get married themselves, I knew my going would distress her as she relied on me so much. However, before this actually happened, one of my sisters, her husband and her daughter, who had been living in Peckham, had taken over the upstairs flat. I must say this was a very big relief to me, as it gave me the knowledge that she would not be entirely alone and that my sister would be there to look after her. Of course I promised that I would call and see her as often as I could, and I did this, but even so, it was a great wrench for both her and me, and caused much sadness.

Chapter Six

"Some Chicken, Some Neck!"
Churchill

Underneath the spreading chestnut tree
Mr Chamberlain said to me,
'If you want to get your gas mask free,
Come and join the A.R.P.'

Oh, war, war! It came upon us at eleven o'clock on a Sunday morning. Millie was preparing the lunch, and I was tying up my flowers down at the bottom of the garden. At five to eleven she abandoned the potatoes and I left the chrysanthemums, and together we listened to Chamberlain's voice coming out of our radio:

> "This morning the British Ambassador handed a note to the German Authorities stating that, unless we heard from them by eleven o'clock that they were prepared at once to withdraw their troops from Poland, a state of war would exist between us. I have to tell you that no such undertaking has been received, and that consequently this country is at war with Germany."

Millie and I looked at each other. This, then, was the culmination of what had been going on on the European scene, but which we had not expected would actually bring us to war. I think it was generally assumed that as we had not intervened over Czechoslovakia, we would not go to war over Poland. We wanted to believe that war was avoidable. Hadn't Chamberlain told us in 1938, after an interview with Hitler, "Out of this nettle, danger, I pluck the flower, safety"? Everyone knew these words, spoken at London Airport, when Chamberlain had come back from Munich, waving a scrap of paper containing an empty promise of peace, and saying the famous words, "Peace in our time".

It was now a year later, and the German promise of peace, and negotiations with the German leader, had proved fruitless, and he had continued to march in Europe. So we were at war. But we hadn't expected it, and we were unprepared, both psychologically and materially. Millie and I shrugged our shoulders, went back to the potatoes and the flowers, and silently wondered what the future would bring. In North London it brought the sound of an air raid siren almost immediately.

"Christ! They're here!" shouted my next door neighbour at me over the fence, and as he was Redvers Llewellyn, an opera singer, his voice bounced not only over our dividing fence, but on and on over all the other fences down the road, vying with the siren which was situated at some distance and therefore not very powerful. Soon all the gardens had an occupant in them who had come out to see what all the commotion was about, and once everyone had established that it was Redvers making all the noise, and therefore no threat, they turned their eyes to the sky. It had to be an aerial attack, for no invasion force could have moved that quickly from the coast. Then the 'All Clear' went, and everyone relaxed.

Thus it was that the 'Phoney War' got under way. During it there was very little activity on land, or sea, or in the air, and Great Britain was able to catch up in building her defences and getting her armed forces into shape. In London, trenches were dug in such places as Hyde Park, and important Government buildings, such as those in Whitehall, were protected by sandbags. Householders who thought they would like one had concrete bunkers called Anderson shelters sunk into their back gardens to protect them from the expected raids by the Luftwaffe.

As I went about my daily business, I came across wires stretched across certain main roads. They were poised about fifteen feet up, the idea being that a fast-moving invasion force could be seriously hampered and slowed down if these wires were lowered at the right moment. Concrete pill boxes were also built at strategic places to direct fire on to the enemy from all points of the compass. Access to our beaches was forbidden, and a pass was required to enter various places. Looking back now, it all seems very ineffective, and a bit of a joke, and we didn't take it too seriously either.

Then Churchill became prime minister, as different from Chamberlain as chalk from cheese. Chamberlain was tall, out of the top drawer, spoke with an upper class accent, and was a bit of a giggle for taking his rolled umbrella with him when he went by plane. Churchill was a big roly-poly of a man, and although equally high born, being a Marlborough, was gruff and stolid. They take their places in my memory as two beads in the middle of a necklace of prime ministers stretching from Balfour to Major. Prime ministers are the country's guardians, and they stand out like solitary sentinels across the years, over and above all other citizens. There they are: Balfour, Campbell-Bannerman, Lloyd George, with his 'land fit for heroes', Asquith with his 'wait and see' policy, Bonar Law, Baldwin, MacDonald, Neville Chamberlain with his famous 'Peace in our time', Churchill's 'some chicken, some neck', Attlee, Eden, forever associated with the Suez crisis, Wilson's 'pound in your pocket', Macmillan's 'You've never had it so good', Hume, Callaghan, Heath, who played the piano, and Mrs Thatcher's 'No, no, no' to Europe. They have all gone, and looking at them like that, the Second World War, during the office of Chamberlain, and then Churchill, who drew on all parties to assist him, and had such giants as Bevin and Morrison in his War Cabinet, is just another episode in the nation's life.

I was too young for the First World War, and really too old for the Second. Nevertheless, I was delighted to be called up in 1943. I went for my medical test in the March, passed with flying colours, and was conscripted into the RAF forthwith. No sooner was this achieved than the really heavy bombing started in London, and very soon the order went out that all builders were required to cope with the damage and debris. So that was the end of that, and very disappointed I was, too. I had been assigned to RAF Ground Staff and was immensely looking forward to joining comrades, just as my father had done twenty-five years before. In the event I joined the ARP, which for some reason or other, which I can't remember now, I preferred to the Home Guard. It seems a real 'Dad's Army' when I reflect on it, all of us dressed up in uniform, training to oppose enemy parachutists, or indeed invaders coming by sea – or in my case, how to fight fires, preserve black-out, and render the community service in the case of being bombed. To carry out our duties, we met at the estate office bungalow near my house.

At the time we felt very advanced, and I suppose we were, when you consider that in the First World War such precautions had been largely entrusted to a single policeman in each district, riding around the streets on his bicycle, blowing a whistle. So, each day I went to work as usual, and was an ARP warden twice over, once in Finchley, and once in George Street. Most nights, I was, to say the least of it, tired. And that was before the bad bombing started. Once it did, wave after wave of air-craft rained bombs upon London. The bomb damage was extensive and many buildings were reduced to rubble. Kimber and James were stretched, trying to repair houses and offices, and sometimes comforting those people whose homes we could not make habitable again. Their sense of loss was pitiable, for in the last analysis, home is all most people have, even if it's only one room, and many of the people we encountered in this situation had only had one room. What can you say when that has gone? What replies would those people who talk so glibly today about shedding the past have ready to give to those people who've lost not just their one room, but perhaps their one son as well?

In some ways, being a builder in the war meant having a great emotional burden thrust upon you which was nothing to do with shoring up walls, or putting in windows. And, in addition, I found it was all rush, rush, rush from ARP duty to building site, to ARP duty to building site, until in the end the building work and the ARP service merged into one continuous task. I hardly ever got home, except to go on duty again, this time in Finchley.

However, there were many people far worse off than I, and I always think nothing is all bad. I was still looking for the silver lining, and I found it in the new contacts, friends and clients I made because of the war. One of these started when St Martin's Church in Trafalgar Square was bombed, and Mrs Donald, an auburn-haired and energetic lady, whose antique shop in Queen Street, Mayfair, we used in connection with clients' requirements, called me up to go and repair the church windows. Mrs Donald was part of the ambulance team stationed at the church under the control of Megan Lloyd George and I was happy to go and see what we could do about the windows. Actually the damage was so bad that all we could do was to make battens and affix dark blackout material to them and fill the windows in like that. An additional disaster for the church was the destruction of their huge golden altar cross, which was twisted and blackened out of recognition. I had to think of something both to maintain the reputation of Kimber and James and to keep up the morale of the worshippers. I got the carpenter's shop to make a large wooden cross, and then I took it home and Millie and I decorated it in gold paint until it looked like the original.

We sat up all night doing this, so that I could present it to the church the next morning, and I think it really did help in a small way to send out the message that we could not be so easily crushed. Afterwards, I went down to the crypt of the church which had been turned into a café where ARP men and women, and other war workers, could get cups of tea and sustaining snacks. I was getting myself a drink when I heard Mrs Donald calling out to me:

"Ah! Mr Gilbert. You're just the man I want. I've got more windows for you to board up for a friend of mine in Grosvenor Square. And after that Lady Louis wants you."

Lady Louis was the elegant Countess Mountbatten, the former Edwina Ashley, and very beautiful she was, too, when I first encountered her. She was extremely attractive in her St John Ambulance uniform, and had a charismatic presence. But all she wanted was name boards! Nevertheless, it was the start of a long association with the Mountbattens which, in the long run, was very beneficial to Kimber and James; it was, in fact, one of my silver linings.

It wasn't long after this that I got my first taste of being personally involved in enemy action. Coming out of Woodside Park Station one evening about six o'clock, I heard the sirens start wailing, and before I could get home a bomb had exploded at the end of my road. It landed right in the middle of the road, and formed a large crater as well as blowing out the windows in all the houses. But worst of all was that it shattered a gas main, and it was several hours before the authorities were able to bring the blaze under control. It was indeed an amazing sight to see these flames leaping into the darkness, a sight accompanied by the fear that our homes would be set on fire, and also that bombing raiders, if they came before the fires were extinguished, would have a floodlit area beneath them.

Soon after this, another bomb came down in more or less the same place and this scattered small incendiary bombs, which lit up the whole street as if it were daylight. Two of these incendiaries were in my garden, and I put them out by throwing water over them which, as an ARP man, I knew wasn't the right thing to do, but in an emergency you just act, and think afterwards.

I knew it was wrong, and it brought home to me there and then that it's a very different thing when you're the one who's assailed by potential disaster. It was with greater understanding that I went back to helping the poor people in the middle of London who were bombed out, and who, even if they weren't bombed, maimed or killed, were under continual strain, sleeping in the Underground or in shelters in their little gardens. But their humour seldom failed. Our sense of 'togetherness' and our determination to lick 'Gerry' were absolutely unshakeable.

We took all the different strategies of the Luftwaffe in our stride. What had started out as straightforward bombing, changed into the tactic of dropping incendiary bombs, the little explosives designed to set fires going and also light up the area, which I myself had experienced, and which were so dreaded, as it was what was to come later when the heavy bombers arrived in their wake, ready to plant their 1000 lb explosives, that put fear in our hearts.

Then we had V1's, commonly called the 'doodle-bugs', which looked, if you caught sight of one, like a little black plane, and whose mechanism was planned so that its engine would cut out at a pre-calculated spot; then it would plummet to earth, causing widespread damage. The next aerial invention to hit us was the V2, which was also a pilotless bomb with wings, but instead of chugging away overhead, it went so fast, virtually ahead of its own sound, that you heard it coming only after it had exploded.

There was a period when things got worse as far as the progress of the war from our point of view was concerned. To begin with, our Merchant Service suffered appalling losses in the Atlantic, and at one stage it was rumoured that we only had ten days' supply of food left. I never discovered if that were, in fact, true. Then, there was Dunkirk, which, even now, hardly bears thinking about, because it was so terrible. And we were alone. France had surrendered. However, we had two weapons the enemy lacked. One was Churchill's speeches, and the other was the Spitfire. I once met an elderly man who told me that, as a Luftwaffe pilot, he feared the Spitfire more than anything else. "*Mein Gott!*" he reminisced. "It could turn on a pin."

After what seemed a long while, the defeat of Rommel by Montgomery was one factor which turned the tide in our favour. So was the entry of the USA into the war, and of course the tremendous support given to us by our colonies, and, finally, the fact that Russia turned on Germany, which forced Hitler to fight on two fronts.

This might not be in quite the correct sequence. But that's how I remember it. And I remember the sense of plodding on. Actually, in my case, I didn't so much plod as hurry from one place to another, for besides going to the office, going to the building sites, carrying out my two lots of ARP duties, and looking after my wife in Finchley, there arrived the additional burden of my mother in her advancing years. She had so often been ill and in pain and not complained that nobody really knew how ill she was. She kept it all to herself. Then, all at once, right in the middle of all this turmoil, she became obviously very ill. I think the terrible memories stirred up by the conflict killed her. She had suffered so much in the First World War, that the Second World War was just too much for her, and she died. It was a great blow to me. On top of it I had to contend with the deteriorating health of my wife. I decided that she just must have a holiday away from it all. A walk in the sea air I thought would do her good. But, lo and behold! I got her to Bournemouth, and we weren't allowed to go anywhere near the sea.

For myself, I found time to join the Masons. Well, I was involved in building, wasn't I? I joined the Red Triangle Lodge in Great Queen Street, and I am a member still, but, I have to tell you, I am the only one left in the Lodge from those wartime days. In addition, for a little relaxation, it was sometimes possible to snatch a few minutes listening to *In Town Tonight*, or *ITMA* with Tommy Handley, Mrs Mopp, Colonel Chinstrap and Funf.

"This is Funf speaking," the character would say, and for some reason we would all think this was terribly funny. We were more easily amused then.

There was also Arthur Askey and Richard Murdoch, who pretended that they were broadcasting from the roof of the BBC, which was a great boost as it reassured us that Broadcasting House was still standing in Langham Place – silly really, but that's how human psychology works. And occasionally there was one of the big bands on the air, or, if you were lucky, you could catch *Monday Night at Eight*. These people did limitless good in the service of morale.

Then, all at once the war seemed over. The knitting circle to which Millie belonged, "knitting socks for soldiers", broke up.

Likewise my two special friends and I would – nostalgically – leave the ARP, and our nickname of "The Three Musketeers" would cease to have any meaning. There was one warden, however, whom I met at this time, with whom I continued to keep in touch. He was company secretary of a big company, and he, like Countess Mountbatten, turned out to be another of my silver linings.

Suddenly, we could breathe again. The war in the Far East still had to be won, it was true, but on the 5th May 1945 delirious crowds gathered outside Buckingham Palace, and the Royal Family and Mr Churchill came out on to the balcony to acknowledge the cheers. Later, Churchill drove around London; he went down Whitehall in triumph, standing up in an open car, giving the victory sign. He had blue, blue eyes, and pink cheeks like a girl's. Astonishingly, after achieving victory, he was voted out of office in the post-war election; the Labour Party was voted in, and Clem Attlee became prime minister. But, then, the populace is ever fickle.

Clothing coupons, food rationing, sweet rationing, and petrol coupons continued to be the order of the day, and everywhere building materials were in short supply. In the end you had to have a licence to do anything. Men were also in short supply. Especially plumbers, which became a crisis in its own right. The great freeze up of 1947 was followed by the great thaw – what was more, it was a great thaw in the days when lead pipes were the rule. Many a householder stopped the flow from his loft with soap and rags applied to the offending pipe, until a plumber could get there, sometimes days later.

The war in the Far East dragged on and the Japs were still holding out east of India and the Pacific Islands, and carrying out their cruel and unprincipled regimes with regard to prisoners of war. Atom bombs dropped on Hiroshima and Nagasaki finally made them surrender, and then peace really 'broke out'. Strange when you think of it that the two countries with whom we were at war now rule us – economically. It's hard for the ordinary man to come to terms with such a situation, and why should he? He's the one that suffered.

So – after all this, what we're left with really is only the memory of the time when we were all united. It's exemplified for me in the song David Croft wrote long after the war was over for "Dad's Army" because in that we're more than united, we're determined to be victorious, too. We in the Home Guard, in the ARP, all of us, warned:

72

"We are the boys who will stop your little game
We are the boys who will make you think again.

Who do you think you are kidding, Mr Hitler
If you think we're on the run?

Mr Brown goes off to town on the eight twenty-one,
But he comes home each evening and he's ready with his gun.

So, who do you think you are kidding, Mr Hitler,
If you think Old England's done?"

And that's my sentiment exactly, German and Jap economic recovery
notwithstanding.

Good old Churchill –
the face of defiant Britain!

Chapter Seven
The Old Puss

Brother Tom had joined Fryers back in 1912, and this was the greatest piece of luck in the world. Of course, we thought it was dreadful when, together with all the outside staff he got laid off some time later, but that, as already mentioned led to his starting up the firm of Kimber and James, because when Mr de Lissa, the owner of Fryers, said he would quite definitely not be allocating any further outside work, we had believed him. It meant, however, that I had been able to join my brother's own company, which I did in 1923, and I had been there five years when we had a second blow: Percy Kimber suddenly died. But, in retrospect, it was fortuitous for me as I was able, at a very early age, to step into a position of authority which I would not have otherwise been able to do.

And it led me to the stars.

Really, it could all be traced back to Mr de Lissa. Mr de Lissa still owned Fryers, and, when the market improved, he found he needed his original labour force, so he came back to us over and over again for the men he had laid off to carry out his schemes. This was only natural, as they knew his methods, what he wished to achieve in the field of artistic decoration, and, what was more, they had been tried and tested as high quality workmen.

Arthur René de Lissa was a star in his own right. He had great imagination and dreamt up one highly original decorative scheme after another, he bullied and persuaded his affluent clients to adopt them, he had all the best contacts in the West End, and he indubitably had considerable business ability.

He was half French, about fifty, very slim, at least six feet two inches tall, and was always very elegantly dressed. He had a deep, attractive voice, spoke with great rapidity, and always charmed the ladies. In fact, he was a real ladies' man. But he had many friends,

Bob Barclay decorating Mr de Lissa's bathroom.

especially in the world of the performing arts, and it was from this source that he obtained most of his business. He rode everywhere in his black, chauffeur driven Rolls Royce, either from his house at 77 George Street, off Baker Street, or from his country cottage at Pinner, which was no cottage but a large house, nor was it a farm, though it was called Mistletoe Farm. He had a manservant called Charles, who looked after him and the house at 77 George Street and after a while a Mr George Blair, recently released from one of the Guards' regiments, who was also over six foot tall and extremely well built, joined the company and never left Mr de Lissa's side. Together they made a very impressive pair, with the chauffeur and Charles always in attendance, and nobody, workmen nor clients, dared say them nay.

As well as his house and farm, Mr de Lissa also had a very large workshop at No. 22 Seymour Mews, W16, which he eventually turned into a garage for his cherished Rolls Royce. He also squeezed in a carpenter's shop, and on the first floor he set up an upholstery department where soft furnishings were made up. His main shop which was open to the public was at 6 Henrietta Street, W1, where he used to sell, among other things, antiques and furniture. But in the main he was an interior decorator extraordinaire, and although most of his clients were theatrical luminaries, many were members of the aristocracy.

Soon after I joined Kimber and James he sent for me, as I was already quite good with paints, and had learnt very quickly how to mix colours. However, this particular job he wanted me to do was not to mix paints but to turn wooden electric light brackets and chandeliers which he had brought back with him from one of his trips to Italy into antiques. He was always up to these tricks, and his clients always fell for them. In this instance I painted the wooden brackets in red tint, then gold paint and applied a little gold leaf. He also brought back brand new wrought iron fire guards, which I had to paint so that they looked old and rusty, and when dry flicked with gold paint, exactly to his instructions. He simply introduced these items into his decorative schemes, which were then bought by unsuspecting clients, and, I may say, sold like hot cakes.

He used to have parties all the time, mostly at Mistletoe Farm. As it was a very old building it easily got knocked about during these gatherings, and I was always being sent for to make good and touch up the various rooms. It often meant painting whole skirting boards, and walls, and rematching the scumbled decorations which were very popular at that time.

As I have already said, we were all nervous of him, and I remember one dreadful incident when we were called to 77 George Street to do some work in the bathroom. It had all just been refurbished, and the walls had rose-breach marble splashers round the top and sides of the bath recess. Our job, or mine in particular, was to mix the colours to paint the plywood bath panel so that it matched the marble splashers. For this highly specialised work we employed a grainer called Bob Barclay, who had gone on to Mr de Lissa's house before me. To my horror, when I arrived and opened the bathroom door, I found red paint all trodden into the new blue carpet that had just been laid. Bob said he was putting out the paints for me ready to mix when he had accidentally knocked a pot over. What was worse, he didn't seem to think he had done anything very reprehensible, but I lost my temper and told him a thing or two. And although we both set about trying to get the stains off the carpet with turps and everything else we could think of, in the end we had to tell Mr Spring, who was Mr de Lissa's head salesman. He would have none of it, but that the carpet would have to be replaced, which it was, and it was Bob Barclay who had to pay for it.

You could say Bob was a good tradesman, but a dirty worker – a very dirty worker. Mr de Lissa would never have forgiven us, had he known anything about it, and we always had to bear in mind that commissions were hard to come by; Mr de Lissa could take his work elsewhere, and we could all be unemployed because of a workman's carelessness.

However, in the main I got on all right with Mr de Lissa, especially when it was a matter of colours. In that field, he and I were certainly on the same wavelength, and for myself I liked trying to come up to his exacting standards and fulfil his requirements. One day, in this respect, he came up to me with a huge bunch of gladioli.

"Here you are, Gilbert," he said, handing me the flowers. "I want six pattern boards painted in colours to match these."

I did the colours for him to his satisfaction and he beamed at me and went off smiling. I found out afterwards that he wanted the colours for a new house he had just bought for himself in France.

I shouldn't criticise him. It was through Mr de Lissa that I got to meet so many interesting people. Laurence Olivier, who called him 'an old puss', was one of them.

"Some of Us are Looking at the Stars"
Oscar Wilde

In 1936 we had an enquiry from Fryers to estimate decorations for a house at No. 74 Cheyne Walk for a young actor. His name was Laurence Olivier. My brother asked me to go with him to measure up and help in the presentation of the estimate. We sent the estimate in. Nothing happened.

Months later, out of the blue, a message came from Peter Jones asking me to meet Laurence Olivier at No. 74 Cheyne Walk. Again decorations were required. I thought about this for some time. I had already estimated decorations for this house for Fryers; now I was being asked to do it all over again for Peter Jones. In the end I decided to go.

I met Mr Olivier, as he then was, and he asked me to estimate decorations for exactly the same scheme I had already prepared for Fryers, but this time to submit the estimate through Peter Jones. However, in fairness to Fryers, they were told what was happening.

Needless to say, Mr de Lissa was absolutely furious and told Mr Olivier that Peter Jones were only drapers, not decorators, and how dare he copy his schemes and ask another firm to carry them out.

We gave the same estimate to both firms. Fryers added 33.3% on to our price, and Peter Jones added 10%. It, therefore, looked as if Peter Jones, who obviously worked out cheaper, were going to get the work. But Mr de Lissa, a very shrewd businessman, arranged to meet Mr Olivier and offered to reduce some of the items, which brought the price down, and Mr Olivier therefore gave Fryers the job.

We started work. It didn't matter to us for whom we were working, except that Fryers' own carpenter was sent to do the carpentry, and we were not allowed to use our own man.

During all our time at No. 74 Cheyne Walk I didn't meet Mr Olivier again, but I did meet his wife, Jill Esmond, on two occasions when we were working there, and she was very nice to me and the workmen.

When I eventually saw Laurence Olivier again he had been knighted, had got divorced and had married Vivien Leigh. One day I was asked by Peter Jones to go and meet him at Durham Cottage, his 'darling place' as he called it, which is in Christ Church Street, Chelsea, and to which he had moved from Cheyne Walk. He wanted me, I was told, to estimate for some work, but I knew it couldn't be for decorations, as during the war, which was then in progress, no one was allowed to decorate unless they had first obtained a licence. Peter Jones didn't know if Sir Laurence had a licence, so I went there to find out, and it turned out he was not in possession of this important document.

However, it wasn't decorations he wanted.

I arrived about ten o'clock in the morning, and was told by the housekeeper that Sir Laurence and Lady Olivier were still in bed, but that I wasn't to worry about that as they would see me nonetheless, and would I go up, please? They were in bed in the top bedroom, which had a large lay-light in the ceiling. What they wanted was for me to board in the lay-light so that during the air raids they could protect themselves from flying glass and shrapnel, but to do it in such a way that the boarding could be removed when no attacks were taking place. I immediately advised against this, and told them that they should move to a lower floor and sleep there; where they were was far too exposed. I realised how dangerous it was, and at the same time how truly beautiful Vivien Leigh was, but I did not allow myself to be distracted.

"What about flying glass, and shrapnel?" I asked. "Worse still, what about bombs?"

"Ah, but you see," replied Sir Laurence, "we like it up here under the glass light."

"But it's very dangerous," I said.

"That may be," Sir Laurence said, "but we like to watch the stars at night. We like to be able to see the sky."

As I turned to go Sir Laurence said to me:

"Just a minute. Haven't I seen you somewhere before?"

"Yes, sir," I replied, "at 74 Cheyne Walk, sir. We estimated decorations there a long time ago, sir."

"Yes, indeed," sighed Sir Laurence, and he seemed very sad when he considered it. "That's it. *Now* I remember."

And the next time I had to go to Durham Cottage, where we were polishing several pieces of furniture, he and Vivien Leigh had, I noticed, moved to a lower room in which to sleep, so they had evidently taken my advice.

I did not see Sir Laurence and Vivien Leigh for a long time after this as they were in America making films and on the stage, and only came back to England occasionally. When I did however, in 1955, he had moved from Durham Cottage to a flat at 56 Eaton Square, and it was there that Adrienne Spanier, who was a theatrical designer and who was attached to Peter Jones, asked me to go with her to meet him. Sir Laurence and Lady Olivier had moved there after they had returned from the States, and we were again asked to estimate for decorations – and this time it was Peter Jones that got the job! There was always an awful lot of competition for this type of high-class clientele. We were not allowed to touch Vivien's bedroom. She wanted the walls draped all in plain cream material, and this was specially made by Peter Jones, and hung by their own men. However, we papered Sir Laurence's room in blue Japanese silk wallpaper, and the sitting room in cream Japanese silk wallpaper.

All the time we were working, there, an American manservant whom they had brought back with them from the States was in residence. This man was very fond of the girls, and he kept asking me what kind of night life he would be able to find in London. He seemed most disappointed when I was not able to provide him with information on this particular topic, and looked at me as if he thought I were deliberately withholding such information, or else was very odd because I did not know.

In the end I said, "I really think it would be much better for you to go out and find out what it is you want to know for yourself." And this, I believe, is what he did, but I don't think he forgave me.

Mr Stardust

My next film star was Stewart Granger. Over six foot one tall, well built, good-looking, very smart, dashing and attractive, he was a jolly nice fellow – most of the time. But he could be unpredictable in so far as he descended upon you when you least expected it, and sometimes in the things he wanted. And, if anything went wrong, expressing irritability came easily to him; I suppose it was because he was an actor.

We met him through Mrs Donald at the time when he had just taken a flat in Thorney Court, Kensington, and said he wanted the whole place redecorated from top to bottom in the current fashion of delicate colours. Accordingly, we stippled the drawing room pale green, the bedroom pale pink, painted the hall and corridor in cream eggshell gloss, and papered the rest of the rooms. So far so good.

But when we got to the bathroom, things started to happen. He suddenly put in one of his appearances when we least expected him, rushed around the flat like a whirlwind, and brought the painting of the bathroom to a halt before we had begun. None of your whites or creams or soft pinks here. He said it was all to be painted dark blue and black. Well, I was shocked, and thought it a bit odd. I ask you, a black bathroom! Very daring and modern, and quite unlike the character in the film he was making at the time, which was *The Wicked Lady* with Margaret Lockwood, James Mason, Phyllis Calvert and Michael Rennie at Hammersmith Studios, not far away. Anyhow, we went ahead, and when it was all finished he came back to inspect it and said, yes, it was all right, but what he had really wanted was a toilet installed between the basin and the bath. Well, he might have told us that before we had decorated; for a start, it meant spoiling some of the work we had just done. Then another complication arose. The four inch cast iron soil pipe, which we needed to connect up, was three foot six inches off the floor, much too high for us to connect a new toilet to without getting the water turned off, but when we applied for permission to do this to carry out the work, the landlord of the block of flats wouldn't hear of it.

"What? Turn the water off for a day, a whole day! Do I hear you correctly? Are you asking me to shut down the water for a whole day and render the block unusable? Have you any idea what my tenants will say? You can't be serious. The idea is preposterous. Out of the question. It can't be done!"

He went on and on, and if he wouldn't give permission, then he wouldn't give permission, and no one could make him.

I explained the difficulty to Mr Granger, but he was also adamant. He wanted a toilet in his newly-painted bathroom. In the end the problem was solved by building a platform, with steps, to the required height, fixing the toilet on top of it and connecting it to the soil pipe behind. Although Mr Granger had agreed to this being done, I was apprehensive about his first inspection of it, but when he saw it he expressed himself well pleased.

"I shall feel like the King of England on his throne when I sit on that," he said, and the toilet and his description of himself on it seemed to amuse him greatly, for whenever I met him he always referred to his feeling like royalty whenever he used this installation.

But he was certainly unpredictable. One day he asked us to stop work on his flat and immediately take ourselves round to his ex-wife, who was Elspeth March, as she had some work that had to be done very urgently. I thought something untoward had happened in her flat, but when I got there with my painter and carpenter she merely wanted a TV set to be installed, and hidden, in her bedroom. Fortunately, there was a cupboard in her bedroom, so we were able to make a low table with castors on it, put the TV on top of that, and adjust the cupboard so that the table could be wheeled in and out as required. I would have thought this was the sort of job that could have waited its turn, but he had to have it done immediately, which was surprising as the lady was no longer his wife, but I have to say that he and she seemed to be on the most excellent terms.

He did not seem to be on such good terms with his sons, or so he pretended, when he moved from Thorney Court to Mount Street in the West End. He sent for me from there and said that he wanted a huge wardrobe built to take all his clothes, and, as he had an awful lot of them, it was going to have to be a very big wardrobe indeed. The carpenters were just nearing completion of this enormous piece of furniture when Mr Granger turned up, as always, arriving just before we had managed to complete whatever it was we were doing, so that he could stop us in our tracks and change something in the nick of time. On this occasion he wanted Yale locks.

"I want Yale locks fitted to all the doors of that thing. I want them so that I can keep them locked and stop my sons pinching my clothes."

It's difficult to fit Yale locks to wardrobe doors, as can be imagined, but he insisted, and I had learnt that, once Mr Granger got an idea in his head of what he wanted, nothing would be able to move it. So, with readjustment, Yale locks it was. However, I did make him change his mind over one idea he had. This was one never-to-be-forgotten occasion after we had finished work on the Thorney Court flat. It so happened that after we had completed the decorations Mr Granger could not move in because of his commitments. Therefore the place was left empty for several weeks, with the result that some of the work, chiefly the window sills, were covered with dust. One day when I returned to the office there was a message on my desk to say that Mr Granger wanted to see me instantly. I hurried to Thorney Court and when I arrived there he was in a fine old temper, walking up and down, and swearing alarmingly.

"Look at the bloody place!" he shouted at me as soon as I put my head round the door. "You're supposed to have painted it. It's filthy! You expect me to move in here, when I've paid you to get it all cleaned up and decorated?"

He looked as if he were going to explode.

"Well..." I said.

"Don't interrupt me," he snapped. "Just look at the dirt. You've had weeks to get this place clean, and now I've come back I can't move in. It's not good enough. What have you got to say about it?"

"As I was going to explain, any window sills..."

"They're not any window sills. They're my window sills and your men are supposed to have painted them. It's a bloody disgrace."

And that's how he went on, leading me round the flat and showing me all the dust that had settled on his new paintwork, swearing and shouting until I finally managed to point out to him that no matter how clean and well painted it had been when we had left it, dust will settle in non-occupied premises, but that I would send a man round to clean it all off and wash down.

"You will? When?"

"In the morning."

"Good."

I moved to the front door.

"Look at it," he said irritably.

"In the morning," I replied.

And this time my assurance seemed to mollify him, and he changed back to his usual charming, if unpredictable, self, and told me he was longing to move in and imagine he was the King on his throne.

"His Voice all Cello and Woodwind"
Kenneth Tynan

John Gielgud was tall and handsome, and he had the most beautiful voice in the world. So, naturally I wanted to hear it, and when we landed the commission of decorating the flat he was going to move into, I felt sure my luck was in. At the time we had been working for Joyce Carey, who was a great friend of his, and who had a dear little house in Chesham Street, SW1 which we used to call the 'Doll's House', so we supposed she had recommended us. But it was Miss Spanier of Peter Jones who actually got in touch with us and invited us to estimate for the Gielgud job. I went along to see the apartment, which was a large one with a drawing room, a dining room, four bedrooms, two bathrooms, a cloakroom and kitchen quarters; it was situated in St Stephen's Close, Avenue Road in Primrose Hill, and was to be decorated throughout in off white eggshell.

Already installed in the flat when we arrived to start work, was Sir John's friend and butler, who was one and the same, a man called Charles; and it was Charles who was absolutely in charge of things, and all orders, as we soon found, as to Sir John's wishes were to be relayed through him. Actually, it was quite an easy job to do, and everything progressed so smoothly that I was sure that, if and when Sir John himself called in to inspect our efforts, he would express himself well pleased.

In the event he did arrive one day, accompanied by Miss Spanier, and with Charles in attendance; they walked all round the apartment, but whereas Stewart Granger had always arrived when you least expected him and rushed from room to room like a whirling Dervish, losing his temper and on occasion having far too much to say, so Sir John was the opposite – very upright, very elegant, and very silent. In any case, Charles spoke for him, so it really should have come as no surprise that Sir John himself had nothing to say. Not a surprise, then, but a disappointment, for all he ever said to me was 'good morning'. And that was it. I have read somewhere that in an interview he described himself as a very shy, timid man. So I suppose that is how it was: he was shy. Whichever way it was his voice remained unused and unheard. Stanley Kauffman, the American film critic, could not praise his voice enough: "...what shading, what music... Everything he says is placed as if by divine order." You can read this sort of comment a hundred times, every time he's mentioned. The trouble was I never heard the voice whilst I was working in the flat.

But soon after we had completed our commission in Avenue Road, Millie and I went to see him in a play, for I was determined to hear him. And I was not disappointed. But I was rather surprised, for who should be in the play taking the part of the butler but Charles himself, acting out what, in fact, he did in real life, or maybe he was really an actor, playing at being a butler during the day time. I don't know.

The impression I had of Sir John, and the slim good-looking Charles, and indeed of the creamy-white apartment, was that they were all part of a dream world, just the sort of impression you'd get in a theatre. Even now I have to tell myself that the man I saw was not only famous, but world famous – for his acting, his directing, his film star status, for his whole theatrical achievement, which has spanned nearly ninety years. But he was certainly reserved the day I saw him.

As everybody knows, he was a member of the renowned theatrical family: the Terrys. He was also *the* Hamlet of the century; one critic said that when he performed this rôle never had English sounded more beautiful. Indeed, Michael Redgrave alleged that ninety per cent of the beauty of his acting was the beauty of his voice.

Alas, it was never directed at me.

Clockwise: The author's mother and father, 1914.
Millie's father, Superintendent J. Read, on the flat roof of the Old Street Police Station, opposite the Old Street Town Hall, 1928.
The author as a young man of 24 in 1926, and his wife, Millie, in 1928.

Clockwise: The author's best friend at school, Stan White, aged 16 in 1918. They remained firm friends for many years until Stan died.
The author's elder brother, Victor, in 1920, aged 22.
The backyard at No. 1 Adys Road, East Dulwich, where the author grew up. The family kept the cows here in winter.

Clockwise: Heber Road School. It was here the author and his
childhood friend, Stan White, were once pupils.
Lord Mountbatten and Arthur de Lisa (the "Old Puss") were two
of the well-known personalities that the author has been
acquainted with.

Left: The author in the gardens of
Burwash, 1968.
Above: The authors Ford Fiesta
Automatic-which proved to be a
great success!
Below: The author with Steve
Coppell, the manager of Crystal
Palace Football Club, taken in 1997.

Chapter Eight

Put Out More Flags

"There'll be bluebirds over
The White Cliffs of Dover
Tomorrow,
Just you wait and see."

We all sang it. We all believed it. Recovery was coming. We gave a huge sigh of relief and looked forward. Everything, absolutely everything was, after all, going to be all right. Vera Lynn spoke, or rather sang, for each and every one of us.

And she sings still. Not only on public occasions but on discs and tapes and records. I've got some of them myself. And when I hear her voice singing these words, just for a few moments, all that optimism, and euphoria, and patriotism, coupled with the sense of belief in ourselves because we had fought the good fight and survived, comes flooding back.

I tell you when I feel it most: it's when I come in late at night. But first, before I get home, I stop off to buy myself a piece of fried fish at the Two Brothers' Restaurant in Church End. Once in, I turn up the heating, make myself a pot of tea, cut myself some bread and butter, put my fish out – and put my tapes in. Then, when it's all ready, I sit back in the dimmed light, enjoy my supper, listen to Vera Lynn, and travel back in time to those lovely post-war years, when we believed everything was going to be better.

To begin with, it really was. Kimber and James expanded so rapidly that, within a matter of weeks, they had taken on forty new staff. The war definitely had its up side, and our offices in Bentinck Mews turned out to be well situated to attract lots of people who, now that hostilities were over, wanted work which had been held in abeyance carried out immediately. Added to this were the contracts made during the dark days when nothing could be done without permission and, even if you got permission, there was the burning question of whether you could get the materials, let alone take on the staff to do the job. But the moment the last 'All Clear' sounded attitudes changed, and one of my first wartime chums to ring me was the company secretary of the International Paper Company Limited.

He gave the firm their first big job after the war. I was absolutely delighted when we got this lucrative order for plumbing, decorating, and, to my surprise, a request for a major operation to be carried out to prevent pigeons from roosting on the sills of the company's premises. Before we got down to work, however, he gave us an order to cover the whole face of the building with flags, banners and bunting. All the owners of the buildings were vying with each other to see who could put on the best show. London was a study in red, white and blue. For us, the decorators, it was the most wonderful feeling – to be putting out flags, instead of salvaging homes.

When we had finished this particular company's total requirements, we wondered if it was just a flash in the pan, or whether there would be other really big jobs to occupy all those staff we had taken on, mostly to cope with war damage. Well, yes, there were jobs, and the first was for Lord Delamere, who didn't live in war-scarred London at all, but at Six Mile Bottom, just south of Newmarket, so it was there that I hurried to see what it was he wanted, and it was like a breath of fresh air just to get out of town.

The road into Newmarket from Six Mile Bottom, which was only a hamlet, is as straight as a die, bordered either side by stud farms and absolutely geometrically straight hedges. In the town itself is the headquarters of the Jockey Club, and just before you get to this, off to the right, down Queens Avenue, is Tattersalls, where the cream of racing stock is bought and sold. Anyone can go in and see the thoroughbreds in their stalls, with their stud names pinned up outside, and you can watch the potential buyers asking for them to be brought out for inspection. They are coaxed out of the stalls, groomed and gleaming, tight balls of energy with beautiful shining eyes. Thousands – I suppose I should say millions nowadays – of pounds change hands every time there is a sale. It is a millionaire's paradise. (Though I'm told that Sheikh Mohammed rides around the streets on a bike! Well, perhaps he does. Wealth can be every bit as boring as poverty.)

Newmarket High Street is one long straight street, continuing from the road that leads in to the town, and here the shops on either side take the place of the hedges further back in the countryside. Up past the clock tower are the Gallops, where the strings of horses in training are exercised. Later in the day anyone can walk on the Gallops, including dogs, if they like. The views are wide and gentle as far as the eye can see, and what it sees is green, green, green. Back at the other end of the town towards Six Mile Bottom is the race course, started in the days of Charles II, who loved his racing, and where today's trainers, breeders and jockeys have achieved fame, or not, as the case may be. It's at this point that the punters enter the game, and fortunes are made – and lost!

I used to take all this in while I was in the town getting something to eat, but I was supposed to be there attending upon Lord Delamere, who certainly wasn't in search of fame and fortune; he already had that. What he did want, however, was a bathroom and toilet built next to his bedroom, and this entailed putting in a waste pipe over fifty feet long. Every job has its own particular problems, and this was certainly no exception. But we never allowed a problem to get us down. If we wanted to maintain our hold in the building trade, it was crucial that we were never defeated. If we had been, we would soon have been out of business.

Following on the heels of Lord Delamere was Geraldo, the band leader, who wanted his flat decorated, and at the same time there appeared a Mr Train, who was a Manchester cotton tycoon, both of them with their individual problems. But with these two gentlemen the problem was not technical. I came to the conclusion about this time that every job was going to throw up a problem of some sort, and Geraldo and Mr Train were no exceptions. Geraldo's, as far as I was concerned, was that he wasn't there. He had no sooner given us the job than he promptly took himself and his orchestra off to Southampton, and sailed away on the *Queen Elizabeth* to the sound of his own music and the ship's sirens. It proved impossible to contact him. We couldn't swim half way across the Atlantic with progress reports. This may well have been a relief in one way, for there is nothing worse than somebody standing over you while you work, but it proves difficult in another when it may be necessary to consult a client concerning matters arising out of his commission. Decorating isn't something you can do and hope it's right. You need to be able to get in touch, because it's very expensive to correct if it turns out to be not exactly what the client thought he was going to get. To begin with, it has to be removed before the work can be started over again. And the client never wants to foot that particular bill. Anyhow, Geraldo went thousands of miles away, and there was no way of getting in touch with him.

Unlike Geraldo, Mr Train, the cotton man, hated music. He was an eccentric who couldn't bear noise, and he was much concerned about how this was to be avoided while the interior of his house was being painted. He certainly lived on his nerves, and his attitude was to waver between pleading and demanding that there should be nothing to disturb his peace and quiet.

"Now, Mr Gilbert," he began, "I must make this quite clear from the start. I can't have any noise in the house – or outside it, for that matter." He looked very fierce. "Do you want me to draw up strict guidelines, on paper, or will you do it?"

"That won't be necessary," I replied. "I'll see to it."

"Ah, yes, see to it. That's what you say. And then what happens? I had a man here last week. Whistling! I can't bear whistling."

"I quite understand."

"You do understand, don't you?" He seemed to crumple before my eyes. "You will give me a quiet painter, won't you?" he pleaded. "You see, I can't stand noise. No whistlers. Nor singers."

"Well," I said, as I glanced round the huge room, "I do have an ideal man."

"Oh, good," he said, offering me his hand on the deal. "Just one quiet man."

"But," I had to continue, while holding his hand in mine, "this is a very big house. One man can't possibly do it on his own. It will require at least two men. I can let you have the man I have in mind. But he will have to have an assistant; otherwise, he'll never get it finished."

"Oh my God!" He jumped back, withdrawing his hand, as if I had bitten him. "Not two of them, please," he begged. He looked quite unnerved and stood off from me as if I were going to attack him. While I was considering whether I should accede to his request, even if it took months for the work to be completed, he fished in his pocket and brought out a huge handkerchief with which he mopped his brow. I wondered if he were having a nervous breakdown. But he suddenly squared his shoulders, stuffed his handkerchief back into his pocket, came up to me and thrust his face into mine.

"All right, then," he growled. "I'll agree. But only one assistant. One. You hear? And he mustn't sing. Why, Mr Gilbert, do painters always sing? Or hum? Humming's worse. They should be brought back after hours and made to hum. That'd teach them a lesson, eh? Bring 'em back and make 'em hum for an hour with no pay." He chuckled at his own proposition, and then turned to me. "Right," he said. "It's agreed. Two painters. No hummers. No singers. No whistlers."

We shook hands on the bargain, and it occurred to me afterwards that perhaps this was his way of doing business, a way of making certain he got what he wanted. He must have known how to get what he wanted; otherwise, he would never have been chairman of an international business.

Anyhow, I provided him with two silent men, and they painted as silently as Trappist monks. The energy they conserved by not using their vocal chords must have gone into their paint brushes, for Mr Train pronounced himself delighted with them. He appeared more and more happy and relaxed each time I went down to inspect the progress of the work, and in the end he was inviting me to take home huge bunches of flowers picked from his enormous garden. It became a sort of pleasant weekly break, with lunch and flowers and sherry.

This all went on for weeks, and eventually the work was completed, and Mr Train expressed himself more than happy with everything, especially the two silent painters. But I came to the conclusion that he was definitely eccentric, for, as I took my leave of him for the last time, he told me that now that the work was done he was going to sell the house and move. As the interior had been in excellent condition before we started work, I honestly couldn't fathom why he was putting himself to so much inconvenience and cost. Needless to say, I never found out.

It was about this time that a change was beginning to come over the big London shops. Try as they might, they didn't seem to be able to get back to their pre-war atmosphere, especially shops like Marshall and Snellgrove, which catered for a particular kind of genteel clientele. At the time no one associated the fact that they seemed to be going downhill with the new mood that the Fifties was ushering in, and which, of course, came to fulfilment a decade later with the free

Sixties. These shops had been tokens, an integral part of that confident, solid way of life when Britain was the supreme nation that the rest of Europe and the dominions and colonies looked to as an example to be followed. Gradually, as Britain's influence declined, so the big shops declined with it, and a lot of them have now gone completely – Swan and Edgar's in Piccadilly Circus, Pontings in Kensington, Bourne and Hollingsworth's in Oxford Street.

Thank goodness, Peter Jones is still there! It was after the war that, in association with Peter Jones, we started accepting commissions that took us further and further afield, first out to places like Godalming in Surrey, and then as far away as the west of England. It became our practice to send out a team of men under a foreman, and it's on one of these jobs that we lost a craftsman. Losing workmen is an occupational hazard. Sometimes they get 'stolen', and it was Colonel Glynn, the Conservative MP, who filched one of our best carpenters while the man was on a job in Dorset. The fact that we were based in London and that was where we recruited our staff, meant that you would hardly expect such a thing to happen. But it did.

Colonel Glynn had very strange ideas about carpentry, and one of them was that he wanted fitted wardrobes, but he didn't want them fitted to anything. Therefore, they had to be specially made to fit into the space available as if they were fitted, but the backs and sides had to be made of plywood, so that in reality the wardrobe was free-standing. Colonel Glynn had just bought a house in Dorset, much too far for our workmen to journey to daily from London, so I sent a team down there and he said he would provide them with camp beds and that he would let them cater for themselves in his house. When they returned, the work having been completed, they were a man short.

"Where's Bob?" I asked the others.

"Oh, he's not coming back."

"What?" I retorted.

"No," they told me. "He's not coming to work here any more."

"What do you mean?" I asked them.

"He's just not coming," they said, and that was all I could get out of them.

It transpired that the Colonel had enticed Bob into his own employ by promising him a cottage on his estate. I never did see Bob again, and I understand that the only thing our best carpenter came back for was his wife and family.

That was one setback connected with Peter Jones, because Colonel Glynn was their contact, but it wasn't the only one. All of a sudden, after working amicably with them for many years, they ceased to give us any work at all. They kept asking us for estimates, but these were never followed up with firm orders. In the end, we investigated and it was discovered that Peter Jones had changed their personnel, and Kimber and James' estimates were being used to give the work to other contractors. When this was verified the staff concerned were dismissed, and Kimber and James were reinstated, I am very pleased to say.

About this time, too, one of the most fascinating places we worked at was Mongewell Park in Berkshire, which, hard to believe, had a large lake in its grounds which was part of another equally large stretch of water that went right under the road and surfaced in Carmel College. It was very big, and the water was controlled by very strong sluice gates. The lake, when it emerged in Mongewell Park, was home to many kinds of birds, and whole flocks of geese sometimes rested there. The owner of this property hired us to put in huge sliding glass doors so that the lake could be viewed more advantageously. Just as we finished this there was a bad storm, and as the sluice gates needed repairing the road was all flooded. The owner asked me to get them repaired as soon as possible, so I contacted our engineer, who was luckily able to put things right, or I don't know what would have happened to the traffic on the road above.

Really, one never knew what was going to happen next. One day I was checking materials, and the next I was puzzling my brains as to how to shore up a Victorian building. This happened when the Middle East Association (an association which introduced Middle Eastern countries to firms in this country for trading purposes) expanded so rapidly after the war that we were called in to re-jig its premises at 33 Bury Street, which also encompassed six shops, into the association's headquarters. It was very heavy work, requiring the insertion of large RSJ's to support the upper floors, and this operation was done not by us but, most appropriately, by a giant of a man, a Mr Mansergh. He had once been a heavy weight amateur boxing champion and weighed over fifteen stone, which was just as well as he needed all his strength for the task. After he had put in the joists and we had made good and decorated, King Hussein of Jordan opened the building officially.

Life, then, after the war, was exhilarating. Even more so when football started up again.

Unfortunately, my team was in the Third Division, but I didn't let that worry me. I was delighted to be back watching the 'Glaziers' as they were still known then. Everything was going well, and while I was building a glasshouse on a client's flat roof in Cadogan Street he got so carried away about the prizes he had won for his flowers that he invited me in to see his cups. While I was there, I noticed photos of Lord and Lady Mountbatten on his piano, and it turned out that he had been Lord Mountbatten's equerry in Malta, which was a big coincidence, as I had just been called down to Broadlands, the Mountbattens' country house, on a 'secret job'.

Chapter Nine

Oiling the Wheels for Merry, Spring and Charlie Brown

Charlie Brown was a foreman, a very good foreman and a very nice chap. And I mention his name only as a representative of all the foremen I have dealt with, and as a preliminary to asserting that foremen are a very special breed. They are the link between the boss, the men and the client; and they can make or break a job, so they need careful handling. As the years went by I got to know all about them, as individuals, their strengths and weaknesses, and how to get the best out of them. The ability to pick the right man for the job is not as easy as it appears, and a lot of judgement is needed if success is to be achieved. The first thing to do is to look at the job and the client, then at the director in charge of the job, and finally select a foreman. Having done this, you must keep the wheels well oiled, so that everybody feels your choice was right, and nobody gets unhappy.

I worked out quite a number of different schemes to keep the staff loyal and contented. One was to allow the leading foremen to participate in the firm's bonus scheme, which, if business had been good, was paid to them at the end of the financial year; and, in addition, we rewarded them in accordance with the profit each job made.

The men got their reward when they went on holiday. We also always tried to make up a man's pay, if we could, when he was late or absent, owing to his own or his wife's illness. We also tried never to refuse a request from a workman for a sub to buy something special, and this was not at all easy to arrange if the repayment period ran into the slack period. But it generally paid off in the long run. If you treat a workman kindly, he will almost certainly repay you with loyalty.

Sometimes, very occasionally, the client rewarded the men himself, as a Mr Harman did when our men proved trustworthy. Mr Harman was the owner of a huge antique lantern light which was condemned, and had to be removed and replaced. We got a new one made for him, but as work progressed he got more and more anxious that, during the removal of the old lantern and the installation of its replacement, his premises would be easily penetrated by intruders and his valuable painting collection put at risk. The foreman and I promised him that his premises would be properly secured and that the men employed there were quite trustworthy. When he found at the end of the job that all had been as we had said it would be, he was so pleased that he gave each of the men a very substantial tip, much more than they were ever used to getting, and they were absolutely delighted.

This sort of gesture was, naturally, greatly appreciated by those who had been on the job, but over and above that, and much more valuable, was that it rebounded on to the firm. One episode like this allowed us to retain teams of excellent workers, who, proud that their honesty and workmanship had been recognised, redoubled their efforts to give of their best.

In order to preserve this relationship between the client and the men, and even more important, between the client's own staff and the men, wherever we happened to be working at Christmas we extended our thanks for their co-operation to people such as cooks, butlers or clients' representatives, whoever they happened to be. This usually took the form of chocolate or wine, but sometimes we gave cash presents as well, and although it was a lot of extra work it was well worth while.

Occasionally, this procedure was reversed and I was the recipient. One Christmas when I was looking after Major Chamberlain MacDonald's premises in Williams Mews, Lowndes Square, while we were mending his roof, his wife and daughter locked themselves out. After I had gone to their rescue, the Major's chauffeur called round with a brace of pheasants for me. But, generally speaking, I was not the one in receipt of anything at Christmas.

Unfortunately for me, Christmas is right in the middle of the slack period in the building trade, which is well known for its ups and downs, and the downs are usually to be found in November, December, January and February. This is when the outside painters are laid off. Whereas you might employ forty painters in the summer, you might only need ten in the winter, and, of course, the men were very artful about this. They knew exactly when the slack period was about to start, and you would find them trying to make the job last longer and longer. However, when the redundancy laws came in in the 1970s, we had to change our method of operating, and no longer laid off staff in the winter, but spread our work out among less painters. I don't know why we didn't do this before the regulations came in, as it is a much kinder way of operating, but when you are in a trade you tend to go along with what that trade does by tradition.

Nowadays, every college, institute, polytechnic and university in the country offers would-be business tycoons courses in business management, among which there will almost certainly be a section on how to handle personnel. But in my day you learnt the art of being in business as you went along, and the busier you got and the more work you took on, the quicker you had to learn. In the 1950s Kimber and James expanded so rapidly that my feet hardly touched the ground – except on Fridays. Friday was meeting day, the day when the directors and the foremen met to discuss the work in hand, and the new jobs in the pipeline.

By now we had devised a system of management whereby my brother, Tom, and I, plus our two directors, Mr Merry and Mr Spring, had our own clients, and our own separate teams of painters, carpenters and other trades, and it was at management meetings, that arguments, if arguments there were going to be, arose, invariably over trying to pick a team for our own jobs.

As soon as the meeting got under way and the topic of foremen came up, Merry would start showing signs of agitation. Merry was an anxious man, anxious about everything, and that included getting a perfect job done. For a perfect job you need perfect workmen, and when it came to foremen, brother Tom had the best foremen in town. After several false attempts to interrupt, Merry would finally get his words out in a rush:

"Can you let me have one of your foremen for a week?"

"No," Tom would say, for his foremen were invariably working on his own jobs.

"Why not? Only a week."

"Because I need them. That's why not."

"But you know I've got a special job to do this week."

"I know. I know," Tom would reply. "I know. And I've got a special job, too."

"It can't take a whole week. Can we share?"

"No. I need them for the whole week."

"Oh, be fair," Merry would continue, and trying to be determined he would name the foreman wanted. "Please let me have Barclay. Let me have Barclay," he would barter, "and I'll let you have Lawler to replace him."

"No."

"Why not? In some ways Lawler's better than Barclay. And clean. Lawler's very clean," he would try to persuade, and then warming to his subject he would get carried away, and bring in irrelevancies. "Look at the dreadful mess Barclay made in Mr de Lissa's bathroom."

Though this had nothing to do with the discussion in hand, nevertheless Tom would look distressed, for it was true that Barclay had made a mess in Mr de Lissa's bathroom. And one that Barclay had had to pay for. As has already been mentioned, Bob had put out the paints for me to mix and had knocked a tin of red on to Mr de Lissa's new blue carpet. It was something Tom was not pleased about, and didn't like to have mentioned.

And while the unfortunate episode concerning Mr de Lissa's carpet danced in the air between us, Tom would become more and more adamant and Merry would shrink back into himself, twitching nervously and being quite unlike his name. Actually, he was so nervous that he was unable to drive into London to work, and having no car on hand at the works, he had to visit all his jobs by taxi. But he was a really good director over all, and it was only his desire to produce an one hundred per cent job that made him put in his request for one of Tom's foremen. In the end, I would usually say that on that particular job Mr Merry could have one of my foremen, and that resolved the matter for the time being.

Sometimes it wasn't the directors who wanted particular workmen. Sometimes it was the client who demanded a particular favourite, and if such a request could be accommodated and the man drafted into the team carrying out the specification, it would ensure that the estimate was accepted. It could equally be guaranteed that if it were one of Merry's jobs, Mr Spring would see fit to complain. He was quite different from Merry, highly organised and always in the office by

8.30 a.m. Far from being nervous, he would thump the table and stare all round, finally fixing on me, as if I were to blame.

"He always gets what he wants," he would accuse me. "Now he wants Wood."

"Well, it's really the client who has asked for Wood," we'd tell him.

"Same thing," Spring would reply.

There'd be a long pause.

"Well, let's consider a compromise," I'd suggest. "Let's think about it. I'll take a new man into my team, and Wood can go into Merry's team – just for this time. That won't make any difference to you. In fact, you could have the painter whose place Wood will be taking. That'll give you an extra pair of hands. How's that?"

"All right," Spring would agree, and I could envisage two or three months without my best scumbler, for, sure as eggs are eggs, the disputed workman would be a master of his craft, and naturally whoever 'owned' him was reluctant to let him go, and I was no exception. But, anything for a quiet life!

Worse than all these Friday meetings were the occasions, quite frequent occasions, when two workmen on the same team decided they didn't want to work together, or didn't like the new foreman, and sometimes nothing would persuade them. Usually, however, they responded to my suggestion:

"Try it for one day. See how you get on. If it's no good come back to me and I'll see what I can do."

I found that, once on the job, like as not, a bond was formed between even those men who had, or thought they had, an antipathy to one another, in which case I heard no more about it. But sometimes my ploy didn't work.

"No, no. I ain't workin' wiv 'im. I'll 'ave me cards."

This was a ticklish moment. I never liked letting my men go, so I usually gave way and drafted the recalcitrant craftsman into my own team, where he could be nursed along until I spotted a suitable niche for him. The men liked that and were always loyal to me out of gratitude for solving their problems. They didn't really want 'their cards', and I didn't want to give them to them, for I knew what hardship was, and couldn't bear to inflict it, not only on the men, but on the next in line, their dependants.

It was like a dance, and one way of getting round it was to take my team into my confidence, so that when yet another misfit turned up they merely sighed and rolled their eyes, but were secretly rather proud of their part in man management by accommodating whoever it was this time. This was all right provided it was a workman who couldn't or wouldn't fit in, but sometimes there was yet another twist to it when it was the foremen who started rowing among themselves, as happened when Tom became ill while work was in progress on the de Vere Hotel.

It was a very big job, and with Tom out of action it fell to me to supervise, but I couldn't be everywhere at once. Therefore, I appointed another foreman, called Jim Hoe, who was a very clean worker and always smartly dressed, to take over at the hotel. However, a supervisor carpenter, Charlie Brown, didn't like the idea at all. He enlisted the painter's foreman, and they ganged up on poor Jim Hoe, who wasn't at fault. Eventually, the situation reached boiling point, and I had to go and make Jim Hoe promise not to interfere with Charlie Brown. After that, I had to persuade the two men and their teams that the new foreman was only there to supervise the other trades – the plumbers, bricklayers, plasterers, etc. Jim Hoe did, in fact, turn out to be not only very tactful, but also an excellent foreman, and eventually they settled down happily together, and the job was a great success.

Unfortunately, Tom never recovered sufficiently to come back full-time, and so Jim Hoe was appointed the fourth team leader, and eventually overseer of all the jobs the firm took on. So it turned out to be a good choice on my part. Not only that, but Charlie Brown proved quite excellent. I had found him in Dulwich, when I stopped to talk to him over a garden wall. He told me he had just been laid off by Higgs and Hill, the big building firm, so I invited him to come and see what he could do for us. After the incident at the de Vere Hotel, he and Jim Hoe became the best of friends and Charlie was made a permanent foreman. I often ponder how strange are the ways in which you can acquire staff, and the benefit to be derived from chance encounters of this sort.

One choice I made, however, was not so good. But then, we all make mistakes. This was in connection with a large house we were decorating in Kensington Square for a Brazilian client, the work for which had been estimated at £80,000, an awful lot of money in 1980.

It was agreed that Kimber and James would also put in new central heating, but arrange it through one of the sub-contractors. However, the heating was not satisfactory and the client's surveyor condemned it. The firm who put it in refused to put it right, so Kimber and James's plumbers had to rectify it and we deducted the cost from the central heating firm's account. This firm then sued us for the deficit, but we contested it, as I was sure we would win the case. However, when we took it to court, the foreman who had recommended the firm in the first place refused to co-operate, and in the end we lost £20,000 on the whole job, and I had to boost the firm's funds from my own capital. Needless to say, that particular foreman wisely gave in his notice before he was told to leave, and I was glad to see the back of him, for he had proved not only uncooperative in dealing with his own poor recommendation, but disloyal as well.

Another foreman to let us down was the one who was working on a block of flats owned by Jack Dare, a friend of Mr de Lissa and the brother of the two musical comedy stars, Phyllis and Zena Dare. I had been very impressed with these two beauties when I had met them, as were all the workmen, I can tell you. At first everything went well and we were happily working away on three flats in the block when our foreman inexplicably deserted us. When I went round to inspect the work I found that he had transferred his allegiance to Jack Dare and the decoration of the other seven flats was proceeding under his supervision with a team of men supplied by Jack Dare. But these things happen. You win some, and you lose some.

So, you see, there are foremen and there are foremen. Tall, short, thin, fat, they come from all walks of life, but not many are disloyal. Some are excellent psychologists in the field of management, and to say that these are at a premium is an understatement. Some are clean, and some are dirty workers, some are rough diamonds and some are a cut above the average painter. Some are quick and some are slow, and the quick ones are hard to work for and the slow are easy to get on with. It also has to be said that, no matter how good they may be as part of a team, promoted to foremen some become very difficult, and some, when put in charge for reasons other than competency, are like fish out of water.

And so it was with Bert Kimber, who was slim and fair and always worried. He was not considered a very good workman by the men. Of course, he should never have been made a foreman in the first place, especially as he had no affinity with paint. He just didn't have a feeling for it. But he was Percy Kimber's brother. And when things went wrong, as I soon discovered they frequently did, to add to the complications, he went on the drink.

Early on in his career, when we were working on the Grosvenor Hotel, Victoria, and Bert was in charge of ten painters, he rang the office to say that he had had to stop work because the chocolate gloss paint which had been specially ordered to paint a dado in the hotel's coffee room was no good. He said it was too thin, and would not cover the undercoat. I was sent to find out what was wrong with it, and after I had I looked at it and looked at it, and eventually started to poke around in it, to my amazement I realised that it had never been stirred up. Once this was done the paint was quite satisfactory, as the oil put into gloss always comes to the surface and should be well stirred before use. Bert Kimber, being a painter, and the foreman, should have known this, and he just made himself look silly.

And so he went on, stumbling from one mishap to another, until the day his brother, being at home ill, was unavailable. Bert was all washed up without him, and, what I had long suspected– the fact that Percy was secretly mixing his colours for him, which was a thing no respectable foreman would allow – came to light.

It all became apparent when I was called to a flat in Fifth Avenue, Brighton, by a very angry client. That the colours were all wrong I could see at a glance, for poor Bert Kimber, a good man in many ways, but certainly not in this, just could not get them right. It took me a whole day in Brighton to remix the colours, arrange for the existing work to be blanked out, soothe the client (a very difficult job this), and get his agreement that all was well before I took a late train back to London. I left Bert there with his five painters, but the realisation that he was lost without his brother seemed to unnerve him, and when the job was finished he handed in his resignation.

In complete contrast was one of our younger painters called Alf Webster, whom we made a foreman at a very early age. Where Bert Kimber had been slow, Alf Webster was quick, darting hither and thither, and keeping everyone on the go. He was thin, had a cast in one eye, a broad Cockney accent, and couldn't bear to see anyone unoccupied. He was, needless to say, well liked by the clients, but the men called him a slave driver. We liked him, too, for the jobs he was put in charge of always paid well and were completed in the minimum of time. He stayed with us for many years until he was forced to resign owing to ill health, when we presented him with a gold watch.

Another painter foreman I shall always remember was a little man, Jim Brooks, who was hardly five feet tall, very thin, and never without a cigarette between his lips. He was also, unfortunately, a very, very dirty worker. Quite brilliant at mixing paints, but dirty! Working at his bench, he had all sorts of staining around him, with tins and tubes open to the elements, and nothing was ever cleared away. After each operation I used to chase him and grumble at him, but I was never able to make him alter his ways. His understudy, a man named Fred, weighed sixteen stone, was very fond of his glass of beer, and was as big as Jim was small. Although he watched little Jim Brooks most carefully, and would have loved to emulate him, he was never able to master the art of mixing paints in the way Jim did. But they made a good pair, a sort of Laurel and Hardy, who kept together and supported one another all the time.

I can picture them now, see them working at their benches, cleaning their brushes, standing before me with a tale of woe for me to solve, taking off their overalls, or sitting with their backs to a wall, eating their sandwiches at lunchtime. In my mind, they are like waxworks, which I can take out of storage, dust down and bring to life, as if it were only yesterday I was talking to them in the paint shop. There have been many, many of them; most of them have played fair by us, and in return I have done the same for them, and helped them just a little bit along the road of life. At least, I like to think so.

Chapter Ten

"Mr Gilbert, My Name is Mud"
Lord Louis Mountbatten

Just after the war, when Lord and Lady Mountbatten took up residence at No. 2 Wilton Crescent, SW1, Mrs Donald and I were sent for to decorate several rooms whilst the Mountbattens were away. At this time Lord Louis had two very large cars, which he used to keep in a mews: No. 10 Belgrave Mews, W1. The flat above this mews garage was occupied by his daughter and her husband, Lord and Lady Patricia Brabourne. These premises used to be the servants' quarters of the main house at No. 10 Belgrave Square, and the mews had an exceptionally large kitchen which, under the supervision of Mrs Donald, we agreed to convert into two rooms – not by dividing it vertically, but, as it was twenty feet high, horizontally. We put in a new floor and formed a new bedroom at first floor level, and then we decorated it.

While we were working on this project, Lord Louis was made Admiral of the Fleet, just as his father, Admiral Battenburg, had been before him. I remember that his valet used to have to lay out his uniforms and see that his medals corresponded with whatever appointment or engagement Lord Louis was attending. He had quite a few naval uniforms with different medals on each, and it was a matter of great importance that the valet got the correct medals and the correct uniform for each occasion.

Later on, Mrs Donald asked us to go down to Broadlands, the Mountbattens' country home, to meet Lady Louis, who would tell us what she wanted done. I was at once struck by the lovely old house, a well-proportioned Palladian style building. Set in its own grounds, in the Hampshire countryside, it had flower beds in front, and the River Test running at the back through the estate. The whole of Broadlands was beautiful. It had come down to the Countess from her father, Colonel Ashley (and she also counted the Earl of Shaftesbury and Sir Ernest Cassel among her ancestors). It was lovely to work there and I would have liked to have strolled by the river, but I had come to work. I worked at supervising the men who painted the drawing room off-white, with gold mouldings to the cornice and walls. Lord Louis wanted his study sea blue, and, because he was a naval gentleman, he had portholes for windows, and all along the corridor leading to this room were pictures of the various ships that he had sailed in.

We were also asked to deal with the spare bedroom, but we were asked to be particularly careful about it, and this it turned out was the 'secret job'. A special guest, we were informed, would be arriving soon, but to begin with, we weren't told who it was.

So we got down to work and painted the ceiling, cornice and woodwork off-white, but were instructed to leave the hand-painted wallpaper, which had a floral design, but which, unfortunately, was damaged in several places. Some of the flowers and stems were discoloured and faded, and it was impossible to obtain a repeat of this wallpaper. As Lord and Lady Mountbatten were adamant that they did not want it removed and the walls re-papered, we had to clean it as best we could and repaint the pattern by hand wherever necessary to match the existing pattern absolutely. When we had finished it – and a very good job we made of it, though I say it myself – we were let into the secret; it was to be occupied by the Queen and Prince Philip on their honeymoon.

On my visits to Broadlands to supervise the work in progress I occasionally got the opportunity of walking around the grounds and by the side of the River Test which ran to Southampton Water, and sometimes I used to take my father-in-law with me, who enjoyed the trip enormously, and he, like me, took great pride in our 'secret job'.

When I heard from Lord Louis again it was from Kent. Lord and Lady Brabourne had taken a country house called The New House just outside Ashford. We had an appointment to go there and meet Lord Louis to estimate for this house, and the moment we got there he said to me:

"Now, Mr Gilbert, I would like you to alter the big fireplace in the lounge. Can it be done? I have asked the local builder, and he tells me it is not possible."

"May I look at it, sir?" I replied. "I will look into the matter and let you know later."

The fireplace stuck out by about three feet into the room and Lord Louis wanted it reduced in size. It was certainly a difficult task, for the bricks went right under the floor. I had my cousin, Will Carter, with me, who was a builder, and together we took up the floorboards and thoroughly examined the surrounding brickwork, and came to the conclusion that it could be done by removing the front face of the fireplace, reducing the amount of brickwork, and then making good and rebuilding the front face with new bricks.

"Well, sir," I said to Lord Louis later, "I think, if we are very careful, we can do what you want."

"Good, Mr Gilbert," he replied. "I knew you'd be able to do it."

It was the same when we were sent for to remove the old six foot long baths from four bathrooms. I suggested that, owing to the shortage of water, we should replace these with smaller five foot six inch baths. The water supply came from a tank which was on a steel framed structure outside the house, from where the water was pumped into the premises as required. It was obvious that when the big six foot baths were used, they took much more water, and the supply kept running out. Lord Louis was not so sure that he approved of the smaller baths, but he said:

"Mr Gilbert, I shall go and try a smaller bath myself. Everyone come with me," he ordered.

So we all went into a bathroom, and Lord Louis got in and lay down in a dirty five foot six inch bath which had not been used for many months, as the house had been empty.

"I've got plenty of room," he announced. "Look!"

And when Lord and Lady Brabourne saw it was practicable, they agreed to the smaller baths.

Later on, when we were installing a food lift from the ground floor kitchen up to the corridor outside the best bedroom, Lord Louis had another bright idea.

"Now, Mr Gilbert," he said, "why not make this lift more adaptable? Make it so that it will take heavy things. That way we can put suitcases on it to save lugging them upstairs."

Our lift man interrupted:

"That would not be advisable, sir," he said, shaking his head, and looking at me to convey the impossibility of the suggestion. "It would be far too heavy to wind up from below."

"But let's try it," said Lord Louis, who was as ever enthusiastic about what he wanted done. "I think it's a good idea. We'll try it."

So we got to work and altered the weights. Some weeks later the Brabournes moved in, but as soon as they started to use the lift the staff complained that they could not deliver the food, as it was too heavy to wind up.

Thus it was that Lord Louis phoned me up one morning and asked whether I could come to Kent right away with a lift man to see about altering the lift back to how it had been in the first place. It couldn't wait any longer. I, in turn, phoned our lift man. Fortunately he was available, and so we travelled down to Ashford in my car, had lunch there, and arrived at the house about 2.30 p.m.

Lord Louis met us at the door, and very worried he was, too; in fact, this particular day, he looked quite seriously distressed. But he knew that I would do my best to sort the problem out for him, as I had known him some time and we had a good relationship. It was the same old story; one of his bright ideas had misfired, and although that was nothing new, this time it seemed to have really upset him, and he seemed nervous of what he had done.

"Thank you both for coming so quickly," he said. "I'm in big trouble. To tell you the truth, Mr Gilbert, my name is mud. My family are angry because I got their lift altered. Now whatever can we do? Can we change the top wheel to a larger one and alter the weights? Would that do the trick?"

But my lift man said, "No. It would not do the trick at all. You will have to leave it to us, sir, and we will put it right," which the lift man did.

Lord Louis was very pleased that his family would not be cross with him any more, and he called for the butler and said, "Will you please bring out some beer for the men."

Lord Louis was very nice. When he was in uniform he was very smart, alert and quick, but when he was in mufti he became very easy-going and a different man, trying to be friendly and please everyone. It was while we were decorating the new house for Lady Brabourne that news came through of the death of our beloved King George VI. Princess Elizabeth and Prince Philip were on holiday in

Africa and Lady Pamela Mountbatten was with them as Lady-in-Waiting to the Princess. Lady Brabourne called me aside and asked me if I would mind taking Lady Pamela's dog back to No. 2 Wilton Crescent and giving it to the butler, so that it would be there for Lady Pamela when she returned from Africa. I did this, much to the annoyance of the butler when I handed it over.

I also went with Lord Brabourne to his old home, Brabourne House, in the village of Brabourne in Kent, to see if any of the fireplaces there could be adapted for their new house. Unfortunately, they were all too big, and a marble fireplace that could have been used was far too fragile to be moved, for fear of its breaking. Lord Brabourne's father was dead, and Brabourne House, which was very large, was being used as a school. They didn't need the fireplaces, but they had to be left there, I'm afraid.

All of Lord Mountbatten's family were very kind to me, especially Lord Louis himself, with whom I got on very well, but after Lady Pamela married Mr David Hicks, an interior decorator himself, we did not get any more work from them, and I never saw Lord Louis again, which made me sad.

I was even sadder when the terrible news of his death while he was sailing on holiday in County Sligo in the Irish Republic was received. I just couldn't believe anyone could, or would, do such a dastardly thing. Lord Louis loved Classiebawn, the castle which had also belonged to Colonel Ashley, and which, like Broadlands, had been left to Lady Mountbatten. He loved Sligo, and the Irish people, and always looked forward to his holidays there, which he earned, as he had worked day and night and at weekends for years on end. He always said that his part of Ireland was safe, and particularly disliked having bodyguards, though sometimes as many as twelve policemen on duty were considered to be necessary when he was in residence at the castle.

However, he believed the Irish would never harm him. But they did. The IRA killed him, and not only him, but they also killed his grandson, Nicholas Knatchbull, an Irish lad helping with the boat, and wounded the elderly Lady Brabourne so that she died later.

They can never be forgiven. Never. Not by me, anyhow.

Broadlands.

Chapter Eleven
The Pack of Cards

I have always liked cards. I thoroughly enjoyed organising the whist drives when I was a lad. So, when we started working on the big London clubs, I suppose it was natural that I gave them nicknames such as 'The Ace of Clubs' for The Athenaeum, 'The Queen of Clubs' for the Ladies Junior Carlton, and so on. They had, for me, a make-believe quality, for although I am a very clubbable man myself, they were out of my world. These clubs were places where the club and its tradition were the most important elements. I myself am more interested in sociability. I like the sort of places where people can go and meet other people with similar interests, enjoy a drink and a chat, and be generally supportive to each other.

The London clubs where we did a lot of our business were different from this, hardly sociable places at all by my lights, and far too expensive for the average man. I am talking about clubs like The Carlton and The Travellers, which are frequented by privileged people, very privileged people, whose portraits – eagle-eyed generals in scarlet uniforms, and admirals in their traditional blue – frowned down upon us from the walls, keeping a watchful eye on what we were doing. The gun batteries and naval guns formed a background to the military and naval gentlemen's portraits, and we felt they could be trained upon us if our work was not a credit to us – and, more importantly, to the club.

The Army and Navy was one such establishment. The club had sold its old buildings to Charles Clore for £500,000, and Kimber and James were required to decorate the new building. As it was an entirely new structure, the work was carried out off drawings, which meant that as the plasterers finished each section, so Kimber and James moved in. This was not so difficult as it sounds as, in general, the requirements of all the clubs were very similar, and the first condition laid down was elegance. This involved a lot of polished mahogany and large gilt mirrors, so, whether it was the card room, the library, the bar, or the smoking room, it was all the same. I often thought the large amount of wall space occupied by the mirrors was so that the members could contemplate their own significance and the insignificance of everybody else. But maybe that was not quite fair, for, if you ever did get into conversation with one of them, they were usually jolly nice chaps, and I could never understand why they needed to surround themselves with all these pompous status symbols.

Bucks Club was as different again. It was founded by Lord Buckmaster for retired officers. Card parties were a big feature here, and everything had to give way to them. Lord Buckmaster saw to that. He was a bit of an eccentric, a fiery old boy, full of energy, who used to come in wearing his dressing gown, look round, and say to me:

"Who the devil are you?"

"Kimber and James, sir. Decorating."

"What?"

He would look at me unbelievingly, and I, in my turn, would look at my watch.

"It's eight o'clock, sir. We're just going to start. Kimber and James, sir," I would reiterate. "The decorators."

"Who? Who?" he would reply, as if he had never heard of us, although he had probably been in contact with the office only the day before. "Who?"

"Can we start now, sir?"

"Well, I don't know. All right. But you can only work from eight to ten. We have guests after that. You know that, don't you? And no wet paint. You got that clear? No wet paint. And only eight till ten."

This was because Bucks Club had card parties that went on all night, so it was only at that time, eight o'clock in the morning, until the club opened its doors at 10 a.m., that the painters would be allowed entry, at which time they would be greeted by a smell of dreadful, stale cigar smoke, broken chairs, and chipped mouldings. How we got round these difficulties, especially not being allowed to have wet paint after 10 a.m., I cannot now remember, but we must have surmounted them, or we would have lost the commission.

Later, Lady Buckmaster organised a Ladies' Bucks Club, along similar lines, except that she had card tables for four, and each table was separated by a screen. This pastime proved very popular, and the ladies took it for granted that they would play their card games separated from the men – unlike the tendency of women today, who demand entry into male preserves in the clubs, as well as in other places; but this had not yet come about.

You could say, I suppose, that I supported this attitude in that I belonged to the Freemasons, who were, of course, an exclusively male organisation, and one in which I participated with energy and enthusiasm, especially furthering the theme of brotherly love, relief and truth. I belonged to the Red Triangle Lodge; I attended regularly, studied the ritual assiduously, and, in the end, in my turn, I became Worshipful Master. The day I took over as Master of my Lodge was a red-letter day for me. My wife and I invited one hundred and forty guests to celebrate at a banquet which we held at Frascati's, and afterwards some of us went to the home of a client to drink pink champagne until the early hours of the morning. I have been Charity Steward of the Red Triangle Lodge for over twenty-five years, but at the moment, being ninety-five, I am thinking of giving it up in favour of a younger man.

The Institute of Directors is not a club in the strict sense, but it engenders an atmosphere of camaraderie among its members; at least it did in my day. It is not exactly a place of leisure – more a sort of trade union for directors of companies, to support and help one another in the business world. As a director of Kimber and James, I belonged to it myself, and I also did a lot of work for them. Sir Richard Powell, the Director General, was a friend of Mrs Donald, and the first job she gave me was to paint and panel the walls in the Directors' building. After that, we built kitchens and converted offices in the original house at No. 10 Belgrave Square, and when the Institute bought No. 9 next door, we cut through the walls and linked the houses together. Then we did the same with No. 8. Membership increased so much that even these extra purchases were not enough, so the Institute bought Nos. 8, 9 and 10 in the Mews behind, and No. 10 was turned into a doctor's surgery with an X-ray room, where members were able to have a thorough health check. After a while, the Institute also bought No. 5 Belgrave Square, which had been the home of the Channon family, to accommodate their library and provide extra shelving as well as bedrooms, bathrooms, and a language centre with classrooms. The whole complex just grew and grew, until in the end it became so busy that we were allowed to work there only at Easter and in the August holidays, when the premises were closed.

Nowadays, with purpose-built conference centres offering first-class facilities and the latest in sound equipment and catering, organisations like the Institute of Directors are spoilt for choice when it comes to choosing a venue for their annual general meetings. But in those heady days of large membership there was nowhere to accommodate the membership, except at the Royal Albert Hall. So, the vast arena in which enraptured audiences usually listened to the immortal works of Handel, Bach, Purcell, and other composers, used, one day a year at least, to echo with the voices of experts lecturing on aspects of big business, making statements on the affairs of the Institute, detecting trends in international relations and prospects for the future.

At lunchtime we were presented with drinks and a packed lunch. Brother Tom and I were regular attendants at these meetings for many years, but after hours and hours of listening to speeches and asking questions, we both, needless to say, looked forward to the arrival of the packed lunch and the subsequent moment when coffee and liqueurs were made available. But overall it was most enjoyable. However, all good things come to an end, and after eighteen years, Sir Richard Powell, the Director General, died, and regrettable changes came about. The work we had in hand when he died gave rise to differences of opinion between us and the new Director General, who had contradictory ideas which, although the job was far advanced, would have meant going back and starting again with an alternative style of decor. This was not only very annoying but also wasteful, and finally my colleague, Mrs Donald, and I, therefore, decided to accept no more commissions from the Institute. Unhappily, things got so strained we never completed the work in hand, for, although the contract had not been completed, we both withdrew our labour, despite the fact that the new Director General wanted us to carry on.

It was all very sad. I had never acted like that before. But there you are – with the demise of Sir Richard Powell, our association with the Institute of Directors came to an end.

But it was not the end of clubs. My interest in them remained, and was enhanced when I came upon a fascinating snippet of history, such as that we discovered at the Ladies' Junior Carlton Club in Pall Mall. There, they had a large circular table which Benjamin Disraeli had

used when he held cabinet meetings at his house in Dover Street. I
don't know how it got to Pall Mall, but that's what I was told. I felt it
should have been given to the nation, but none of the ladies seemed to
think it was in any way unusual.

However, I can tell you that their kitchen ceiling was more than
unusual. It was black. I thought it had been painted black, and
considered it a most unusual and inappropriate colour for a ceiling,
kitchen ceiling or otherwise. But, when it was more closely examined
it was discovered to be covered in thick, black grease. It was filthy,
and I shouldn't think it had been cleaned since the day it had been
originally painted. The men scrubbed it off, for which they claimed
'dirty money', and it was found to be white! I am sure it hadn't been
touched from the days when Disraeli was prime minister!

This particular job always held a place in my affections for, not
only did it have historical connections with Queen Victoria's favourite
prime minister, but it also combined two facets of my love of playing
cards – the clubs, and the ladies who brought with them their
diamonds, spades and hearts.

"There is Nothing Like a Dame"
South Pacific

That's very true – there is nothing like a dame, but dames and
decorators are usually a combustible combination. Kimber and James
met them in all sorts of categories: groups of ladies, as in the clubs,
wives of clients, wives with regard to foremen, female clients in
regard to foremen, and even cooks, maids and housekeepers in regard
to foreman. Depending on which set of circumstances pertain, special
links are forged with them. Wives, for example, are often great
'coverers up', and will ask your help, as the paint firm's director's
wife did when she left a tap on and damaged his study ceiling which
we had just re-done. Her husband was not a man to be trifled with, so,
when she appealed to me to do something before her husband got to
know, I had it repainted for her without his ever being aware that she
had spoilt it.

However, in these end-of-the-century equality-of-the-sexes days,
you aren't likely to find wives taking recourse to such an action, and,
indeed, many of the women we came across in the course of our

business wouldn't have done so either. It is just that nowadays we tend to think of women as having only recently struggled out from under the blanket of submissiveness, having been, up till now, handicapped by male prerogative. But don't you believe it – not where decorators were concerned. Many women, especially among the middle and upper classes, knew better than any man how to assert themselves, enjoyed a leisured existence, and had a degree of financial independence far greater than has been commonly believed.

It was the Queen's Coronation that did it. 1952 was, in my opinion, the year which gave the stamp of approval to *women*. There she was in her golden coach riding from the Abbey – *crowned queen*. She epitomised *woman triumphant*. During the war they seemed, albeit illusory, transmuted temporarily into the gentle sex. There was even a film called just that, with Joan Greenwood in the lead. Then there was the delectable Vivien Leigh in bed with her swain, looking at the stars, or the charismatic Edwina Mountbatten being a free spirit, and the fascinating Phyllis and Zena Dare. These, therefore, were the rôle models I had encountered. And each one was a Queen of Hearts, queen of my heart, anyway. True, I had already had my first taste of a formidable lady who was very much in charge, with Mrs Hanbury and her glowing walls; she clearly signalled to all and sundry that as she was paying the piper she would call the tune. But she was the exception, I thought. But I was wrong. After the war, a dozen Mrs Hanburys came tumbling out of the woodwork.

Mrs Baird was the first. She was a very rich Jewess for whom Kimber and James, now established in smart new offices in George Street, carried out all manner of commissions. But she had one abiding obsession, and in between new colour schemes and refurbishments, this obsession, which was to move her many, many valuable pictures round and round her apartment in Hamilton Terrace, surfaced. And who do you think was always allotted this task? None other than I, of course, for no workman, and in her case, no foreman either, was considered capable of the task.

"Jack..." my brother would say as he put down the phone and took in a deep breath, "...she wants them moved again."

He never needed to say who it was or what it was that wanted moving. I just knew. It was a ritual: up the step ladder, grasp the picture, down the step ladder, put the picture on the floor. Then, move the ladder along and repeat the performance with a second picture.

When I'd got my breath, I'd move the step ladder back, lug the second picture up to the empty space, hang it and descend. I would wait, while the clock ticked loudly, and Mrs Baird would twist her huge diamond rings round and round. She would imperceptibly sway from side to side. She would consider the arrangement, while I waited for that dreadful moment when she would say:

"No."

The rings would flash, the diamond earrings would shake in sympathetic agitation with their owner, and the inevitable brooch would rise and fall on Mrs Baird's bosom, twinkling and winking and sparkling in a smug, self-satisfied sort of way, as I stood awaiting Mrs Baird's next command.

"I don't think it's right there," she would say to me, and as if I were at fault in hanging it in the wrong place, she would add, "It will not do. We will try it somewhere else. Yes? On the other wall. The light will be on it. It will be better there." And she would point a long bejewelled finger at a selected place on the chosen wall, and the diamonds would all flash and glitter again. "You see what I mean?" she would say. "Try again."

So I would start the procedure of getting down the picture I had just put up, and all the time in my mind I could see the picture whose place I had just unsuccessfully filled lying on the floor, and by the time I had put the first picture up on yet another wall, there would be two pictures lying on the floor, looking for hanging space. Sometimes she would have all the pictures on the floor at once. It was a nightmare.

But Mrs Baird was Mrs Baird. She had a lot of money, she was covered in diamonds, and her pictures were very important to her. So I persevered, and in the end we got them all back up, looking exactly as they had when I'd first come in; in fact, everything was exactly the same as when I'd first come in, except that I had dreadful backache. Mrs Baird, of course, didn't care a bit. She pronounced herself quite satisfied with what I'd done. She was my Queen of Diamonds.

Barbara Cartland was much more considerate and colourful. Pink! She was my first *grande dame*, and everything about her was larger than life – and *pink*. Her make-up, her negligee, her bed. And it was from her bed that she gave her orders. It was a very large, feminine, frilly bed, with cushions and pillows and papers.

From Miss Barbara Cartland, D.St.J.

CAMFIELD PLACE,
HATFIELD,
HERTFORDSHIRE.

POTTERS BAR (77)
42612
42657

22nd July 1985.

Dear Mr. Gilbert,

I am so sorry to bother you, but

Miss Cartland is anxious to have any photographs

either of yourself or of Lord Mountbatten

taken at the time, and if you have any, she

would be so grateful if you could loan them

to her for her new book.

It is going to be published shortly,

to coincide with the showing of the new film

about Lord Mountbatten.

Thank you very much indeed.

Yours sincerely,

Hazel M. Clark.
Secretary.

CAMFIELD PLACE,
HATFIELD,
HERTFORDSHIRE.

POTTERS BAR (77)
42612
42657

9th April 1985.

Dear Mr. Gilbert,

Thank you so much for your
delightful letter, and it is just what I
want to incorporate in the book I am
writing about Lord Mountbatten, including
letters from people who either met him
or knew him.

Thank you once again for helping
me, I am so grateful.

Yours sincerely,

J. W. H. Gilbert Esq.,
Kimber & James Ltd.,
14 Bentinck Mews,
Marylebone Lane,
London W1M 5FL

Letter from Barbara Cartland.

Barbara Cartland wanted what we had done for Lord Delamere in Six Mile Bottom done for her. She wanted a new soil pipe. So when I went to visit her on her estate near Essendon in Hertfordshire, I wasn't too worried. Lord Delamere's soil pipe had run the length of fifty feet and that was bad enough, but imagine my horror when it was revealed to me that Barbara Cartland's soil pipe was intended to go across a whole field. Well, it could be done, I supposed. It was done. And one of her requirements was that the foreman should report to her each morning about how far the men had managed to dig across the field the day before. Actually, she could watch them out of her window: the men working away with their shovels and spades. So she was my Queen of Spades, and I was rather amused about this, but the foreman, on the contrary, was nervous about the whole procedure, and especially about visiting her. But... she dictated her novels, and he reported the progress of the soil pipe. That's all there was to it. Quite a good working relationship, with both of them doing what they were good at.

Barbara Cartland was a very nice lady, very public spirited, always optimistic, and anxious that everyone should live life to the full. Later on, I had occasion to write to her about Lord Louis Mountbatten, and she sent me back an extremely nice letter. I think she is a wonderful example – positive and bright herself, and finding the best in people, rather than the worst.

Rather like Barbara Cartland, and rather nice, was a very old lady, a Mrs Whitiker, who engaged us to decorate her flat at Rutland Gate. She was also the owner of a furniture shop, and she gradually started to introduce us to her clients, one of whom was Lady Isobel Guinness, who had just bought Westmeads, near Banbury.

It so happened that I had relatives at Banbury, so, on Sunday afternoons, my wife and I used to motor there, and, after we had visited my aunt and uncle, we used to go all posh and take tea with Lady Isobel. She was a charming lady, and years later invited us to come and meet her new husband, who was Lord Throgmorton. He owned Throgmorton Court, which was rather run down, and urgently needed electrical renovation, as the wiring was obsolete, being in wood casing. He asked us if we could do it, but he was so shocked at the cost, he decided against it. I don't think he ever managed to get it done, for eventually Throgmorton Court was handed over to the

National Trust, and Lord Throgmorton and his family were given a suite of rooms in it to live in.

In 1991 I was on a National Trust tour, and was standing in the hall of this stately home when I saw Lady Isobel coming down the stairs. We recognised each other immediately, and were delighted to be reunited all of forty years after I had first gone to work for her at Westmeads. She was just as charming as ever, and she joined 'my ladies' as I call them: the Countess Mountbatten, Vivien Leigh, the Dare Sisters, Barbara Cartland and now Lady Isobel were the Hearts in my pack of cards, and still are, even to this day.

But some ladies I have known definitely don't qualify for this honour. One such was Lady Swansea: she was a very different type of woman, very different indeed. I was calling upon the Swanseas to discuss work to be done, and poor Lord Swansea had forgotten to bring the list of jobs with him; when he came into the room without it she sent him away to get it in a most peremptory manner, making him look small in front of everybody. I most certainly did not agree with it and never liked her for it. Lord Swansea was a real gentleman, and at the time he had just returned to England after winning the Gold medal in the Olympics for his country. To think that his wife talked to him like that! What's more, he did a great deal for charity, and was a highly respected leader in the Masons. He is to be the Provincial Grand Master in 1997, and is looked up to by everybody.

Another lady client who was a bit of a tartar, and in many ways echoed the attitude of Sir Crispin English, was Mrs Wyndham of Grosvenor Square, who was a member of the Woolworth family. Her premises were covered in cream carpet, and you could not enter until you had first removed your shoes. She eyed everyone up and down before she let them in, and I got so fed up with this constant battle over the footwear and the carpet that in the end I bought some suede shoes and left them there to wear when I called. This absolutely delighted her and she changed her attitude to me, but not, I'm afraid, to the men who while working in her house had to wear slippers and white coats, and be very, very quiet. They said a lot of uncomplimentary things about her, and were glad when the job was done.

Like Mrs Wyndham was Mrs Burns who owned North Mymms Park, and whose most important possession apart from this property was a big chow called Moses. Moses was a terror with a mauve

Mrs Burns and Moses.

tongue, and his devotion to Mrs Burns was one hundred per cent. If you went to work for Mrs Burns, you also went to work for Moses. To begin with, like so many of the others I have described, Mrs Burns said I would have to supply her with our best and cleanest workmen and there was to be absolutely no noise. She was very particular indeed, but we satisfied her and the work continued to come in year after year, as she had a couple of rooms decorated in rotation every twelve months. At first, when we had a job at North Mymms Park, I used to call there every morning to see that the foreman and his mate were keeping to their vows of cleanliness and silence, but as the years went by Mrs Burns got a bit more relaxed and would send a message to say that I need not come till the afternoon when she would like to take a turn in the garden with me, to discuss the work in progress. In the end I used to go and have tea with the butler and wait till she sent for me. It was as though we had gone back in time a couple of centuries. She behaved like a chatelaine, with her keys, her servants and her guard dog. Her greeting was always the same.

"Did the butler give you a good tea, Mr Gilbert?"

"Yes, thank you."

"I'm very glad. Now let us walk in the gardens. I'm sorry I can't invite you in. It's the dog, you see. He won't let anyone in. And, Mr Gilbert, I do beg you to be very careful. Keep on my right side – away from Moses. If you stay on my right side, he won't attack you. At least I hope he won't. He's so very protective of me, you know. Now, you start. How is everything going?"

So, we would walk in the gardens, and I would give an account of the work in progress, and all the time I would have my eye on this dog, whose mauve tongue would keep appearing on the other side of her skirt. It never did attack me, however. But it had very large teeth, and snarled from time to time, which made me feel very uncomfortable.

As did Mrs Jefferies' pigeon. Mrs Jefferies lived in Edgware, and she also had large gardens surrounding her beautiful old house, and a lake to boot. Except that she didn't have a dog, she had a pigeon.

Now, this pigeon was, in a way, worse than Moses; it was worse than any dog, because it could come at you from any angle, and you couldn't assess exactly whether it was looking at you and getting ready to fly, or merely taking in the scene and stretching its wings to pass the time. Mrs Jefferies lived alone in her big house, with only a

Mrs Jefferies' pigeon.

housekeeper and the pigeon for company. She never went out, and nobody ever came in. And it was very eerie to go and take her orders and find that you were really taking orders from Mrs Jefferies *and her pigeon*. It used to sit on her shoulder, or, if she should move, follow behind her, and whenever she addressed you it would fix you with its red eye in a most menacing manner. She used to talk about what she wanted done at great length, and from time to time consulted the pigeon about her plans, so that, when you left you had the distinct feeling it was the pigeon, and not Mrs Jefferies, who had given the orders.

While I was there one day, talking to Mrs Jefferies and the pigeon, for she liked you to acknowledge it and tell it as well as her what you intended to do in the way of decoration, a swarm of bees infiltrated her conservatory which alarmed the housekeeper, who, in turn, alarmed Mrs Jefferies and the pigeon. I was all for calling in an expert to deal with them, but Mrs Jefferies was dreadfully agitated, and begged me to get rid of them, which I did, equipped only with a pair of gloves and a box. I was rather shaky afterwards, and glad of the glass of sherry which she fortified me with. But it broke the ice, and after that, the pigeon and the rather frosty housekeeper seemed to regard me with a more friendly eye, and Mrs Jefferies herself started to tell me all her problems, one of which concerned her next door neighbour, who, not very amicable to begin with, was even less so once he had noticed that her fence and gate encroached upon his garden by six inches. I got our surveyors to look into the complaint and it turned out that the neighbour was correct in his assertion, so we re-aligned the fence and gate to its legal position, and after that the neighbour and Mrs Jefferies were on much better terms, and the pigeon and the housekeeper took me to their hearts.

One lady who did not take to me, nor me to her, was the daughter of the Fabers, who lived at No. 4 Chester Square, opposite where Lady Thatcher lives now. The first job we did for them was a straightforward decorating commission of painting the back and front of the house. The Fabers had a large family, of four boys and one girl, and as they grew up they all wanted their own apartments, so Mr Faber bought a mews house backing on to his own property to accommodate them, and we decorated this too.

So far, so good. However, the only daughter got married, and Mr Faber sent me to decorate the house which he had bought for her in Fulham. At the same time as giving me the job he gave me instructions that on no account whatsoever was the amount stipulated to be overspent. But he hadn't reckoned with the fact (or, perhaps he had) that Miss Faber had very expensive ideas, and wanted, as I remember it, tiled bathrooms, new fittings and costly wallpapers.

"I'm sorry," I said to her, "but I cannot do all this. It's going to work out too expensive. It can't be done."

"And why not?"

"I have to have your father's permission for these extra things. They are over the stipulated cost."

"What cost? What are you talking about? I am giving the orders here. And I am telling you to do them."

"No." I was adamant. "It can't be done," I replied.

"You are a bloody fool," she shouted at me. "Now either you get on and do it, or I shall get someone else."

"Very well," I said, and left, taking my men with me.

I was very angry. In all the years I had been dealing with clients, nobody had ever spoken to me in this manner, and to make it worse this was a young person half my age. Have they no respect, and who do they think they are, just because they come from a moneyed family? It wasn't good enough, I can tell you, in my opinion.

When I had recollected myself some days after, I spoke to her father, and complained, not only about the cost of the materials and work she was running up, which was outside the budget he had set, but also about her rudeness. Mr Faber apologised to me, and said that we should leave the work for the time being, which we did. However, it wasn't long before he got back to me and asked me to estimate for the additional cost, which he then agreed, and we went ahead and completed the work.

Shortly after we had left the house in Fulham, the firm received a request for us to go and re-fit the kitchen according to plans already drawn up, but this we refused to undertake. I don't like ill-mannered people, whether they are rich or not. Lady Abercrombie, Lady-in-Waiting to the Queen, whose flat in Pont Street we decorated was never ill-mannered. But then, being a lady born and bred, she wouldn't be, would she? I remember her as being tall and fair and attractive; and she was my last but one personal client. But just before her was Miss Platt of la Belgrave Square. She had a lovely house right on the corner of the Square and Wilton Crescent, a couple of doors away from Lord and Lady Mountbatten. Miss Platt, like Lady Abercrombie, was slim, tall, fair, and very good-looking; she was also well-spoken, highly educated – and modern! In fact she was a thoroughly modern miss, as her title implies. Her clothes were extremely stylish and colourful, she was very rich and independent, she entertained a great deal, and when not at home was usually to be found at the races. Added to all this she had a lady companion, a housekeeper, a chauffeur, and she had *ideas*.

One of these concerned the ceiling in her drawing room, a fine room twenty foot square, with an enriched cornice and panelled walls. She wanted the ceiling painted to resemble the sky. A friend of hers had had it done by an artist, and she wanted it done too. She asked if we thought we could do this, and when I said we certainly could, she sent me down to Leamington in Hampshire to the friend's house, where armed with a box of paints, two pattern boards, one painted off-white and the other light blue, plus a box of stainings, after a great deal of effort, I was able to match the artist's ceiling.

Later while Miss Platt was away, our grainer, Bert Baxby, was able to copy this, and produced a ceiling in Miss Platt's drawing room that looked like the sky. We hoped that it would prove satisfactory in Miss Platt's estimation and, much to my relief, on her return we got a phone call to say that she was pleased with the result. She congratulated the grainer, and, indeed, I have to say, was appreciative of all the men, including me, who worked on this project.

Then came my very last client: Mrs Braby of Eaton Terrace, who just like Mrs Burns and Mrs Wyndham, demanded clean and silent workmen, except that, in her case, having no back door, the men had to enter and leave by the basement. She had a most difficult job done, which was to take out the whole of the brickwork to the front of her house and re-build it. This is doubly difficult when the owner of the house is house-proud and maintains her premises in a state of inner and outer perfection. She was also fussy about the workmen, and could be quite reactionary if she didn't like them. But, strangely enough, she took a great fancy to one of my old painters, a broad Cockney called Bill Meek, and when this man was no longer available Mrs Braby was quite put out, and couldn't be persuaded to accept the replacement, whom she did not take to at all. This went on for some time, and the poor man was, in his turn, also getting upset, when I suddenly hit upon the idea of telling her that this particular workman was the one we directors ourselves used in our own homes (which was quite true), and that he was so trustworthy that, actually, he had the keys to all our houses in case of emergency or, if necessary, to let himself in and out to work. This had a magical effect upon her. She immediately decided that he was the man for her, gave him his own key to Eaton Terrace, and eventually put him in charge of answering the telephone for her, which, I believe, he is still doing to this day.

Well, there you have them, all my ladies, all my Queens of Diamonds, Spades and Hearts, with only one or two exceptions, and then if you add the Clubs, you have the whole pack.

Chapter Twelve
Come the Bad Times

It was a very hard winter. It started early, and the cold had a devastating effect on the weak and elderly. From the beginning, there was mist, wind and ice, and to these snow flurries were persistently added. The doctors' surgeries and the hospitals were overflowing. At work the men could not proceed with outside jobs, and, in many cases, there was difficulty in getting to the jobs in the first place.

But Christmas, everyone agreed, and no matter how distant it was, was approaching, and that cheered things up, for there is always the thought 'once Christmas is over...' a New Year will begin, and everything will be better, and we shall have the energy to tackle those things that aren't. Why we should assume the conclusion of Christmas would improve the weather, or increase our ability to combat it, I don't know. Actually, I suppose it is really a question of having an excuse to put off thinking about the difficulties.

Then, there is the pretty side to it all. The snow, at least when it first falls, transforms the world to fairyland. The Dollis Brook at the bottom of my road looked very dramatic as it swept along, black between its white banks, and the countryside all around, up towards Woodside Park and Barnet, was idyllic.

So, all in all, we gritted out teeth, and plodded on – till Christmas. But, as far as we were concerned, the bad news got there first. One afternoon there was a knock at the door, and, when I opened it, I was surprised to see a policeman standing on the step, a black silhouette outlined against the snow. He told us that my uncle in Banbury had died. That was all. Nothing else. He imparted the news and went.

My wife and I decided we ought to go to Banbury to see what was happening and to console my aunt, but the roads were impassable. However, after much hesitation and discussion, we decided we ought to make the attempt there and then. So I got the car out, and we set off. It was one of the most dreadful journeys I have ever made, slipping and sliding all over the place, and continually having to get out of the car to clear the frozen windscreen. During the journey my wife began to feel quite ill, which wasn't surprising, as that autumn she had had a series of small accidents, each of which had left her rather unsteady.

We eventually got to Banbury, and started to help my poor aunt. It was some days before the roads cleared, and once they did we came home post haste. However, we had hardly got our foot in the door before we got word that my brother-in-law had also died, leaving my sister alone, and that my other sister had been taken into hospital. In the days that followed this terrible state of affairs we were told by the hospital authorities that she wouldn't recover, which she didn't. Her husband was so shocked by all the news we had received, that this was just too much for him to bear; he went to pieces, and he died three days later.

It was a living nightmare.

The year finally progressed towards the Christmas we had all been waiting for, and I thought to myself that when it had actually safely gone, I would breathe a sigh of relief, but before it did my mother-in-law was taken into Barnet Hospital, where she died. It was unbelievable. This latest event meant that my father-in-law was left alone in his Whetstone house but, being of a very independent nature, he was determined to manage on his own and not to worry us. For the first few weeks he seemed to be coping. He was very deaf, but we managed to persuade him to get a hearing aid, which he did, but being extremely clumsy and obstinate, he was really unable to benefit from it, so he was virtually cut off from life. I felt very sorry for him, but he was difficult to help, and, to be honest, I was exhausted.

Well, Christmas was finally upon us. I had seen that all the Christmas boxes to the staff and clients and their employees had been delivered. And I finally got home for a well-earned break. I liked Christmas. I liked the sociability of it. But this particular year, all I wanted was rest. So, I had my Christmas dinner, and – unusual for me – I went to sleep.

The next day I felt better. I am the eternal optimist. The sun was shining, and further snowfalls had ensured that it still looked very pretty when you opened the front door. I went for a walk by the brook, and came back later somewhat heartened. We had lunch on

Boxing Day about two o'clock, and I had just settled down for a repeat of Christmas Day's idleness, when the bell rang. When I went to the door my father-in-law was standing there, with tears in his grey eyes. This great big sixteen stone man, so domineering and strict in his day, so secure in his size and authority that everyone called him Hindenberg, was crying like a child to be let in.

"I can't," he kept saying. "I can't."

I got him indoors and gave him some brandy. His boots were heavy with snow, and he kept saying he was very cold and distressed.

"Can't what?" I asked him.

"I can't. I just can't."

"You must tell us," I insisted. "What is it you can't do?"

"I can't manage on my own," he sobbed.

It was a terrible moment for him. I realised that.

"Well, that's all right," I said. "You must come and live with us here."

"I have had to give in," he cried, and round, pearly tears ran down his face.

I can see them still. His big frame shook with the cold and the tragedy - for him - of having to admit he was no longer in charge, not even of his own life.

"I know I'm no good any longer," he confessed.

I felt very sorry for him, and my wife and I tried to cheer him up, and make light of it by ignoring it, and by the end of the day he was feeling a little better.

But he was never able to go back to his own home again, and he was eventually confined to the house. But we managed somehow, and he lived with us until he died.

It was the most awful Christmas I can ever remember.

The strain of all these events, and looking after her father, as well as still going to the office, took its toll on my wife, and she started to have more small accidents, one of which was to break her thumb. It was while she was getting this attended to that she was suddenly taken ill with severe stomach pains and had to be admitted immediately into hospital for a major operation. After the operation, she was sent to another hospital for radiotherapy for two months. But she recovered, and eventually went back to the office for another three years, before she was forced to give up altogether.

128

As time went on, she got more and more unable to cope with going up and down the stairs, so I got in one of my men to make alterations to the house, including the installation of a downstairs toilet, and this was a great help.

But there was a bonus for me in all this unhappiness. My brother, Victor, decided to move back to London. So, after many years, I again had someone to go to the home games with at Crystal Palace. It was lovely, and it was a good period in the team's fortunes. Malcolm Allison was manager, we had girls entertaining us on the pitch to start the matches off, and Johnny Byrne was playing well, and eventually got transferred to West Ham for £65,000, an unknown figure in those days. I must say I thoroughly enjoyed every minute of it, especially as I now had my brother sitting next to me in my seat in the main stand, which I had occupied for more years than I cared to remember. Suddenly, I felt that everything was going to be all right again.

"Here, if I am Not Mistaken, is Our New Client"
Sir Arthur Conan Doyle

That year, after our dreadful Christmas period, work, perhaps because of the weather, was scarce, and the directors of Kimber and James realised that it was a matter of urgency to find new clients; if they didn't, they wouldn't be able to carry on. It was, indeed, a worrying time because clients seemed to be few and far between, but, come the spring, things picked up. As is the way of such occurrences, once one new face appeared, a succession of new faces followed at our office, asking for jobs to be done.

Some of these were rather difficult, but if you were in business you had to be ready to meet the challenge, so, when a client entered the office with a request, the response from us was never to consider *whether* we could do the job, but always *how* we could do what was required. There was never any question of our turning work down because of the difficulties it might entail. Rather, it was a challenge we were determined to meet and overcome.

One odd job the firm was asked to do was to provide a bathroom in the well hole running through the centre of a house. I never, in a thousand years, thought the local district surveyor would approve the plan, but he did. Our problem was how to construct the thing. A piece of paper with a drawing on it is one thing; to get to grips with bricks and mortar and pipes and fittings, not to mention plumbing and soil pipes, is another, but in the end we got the job done to everyone's satisfaction.

Another of our clients at this time, a Mr Galliers Pratt, made an even odder request, which was to have a kitchen built into the bow window in the corridor of his flat at 101 Mount Street. On the face of it, this would seem to be impossible, but I said we would see what we could do, and in the end we managed it by putting cupboards on either side of the window, installing a stainless steel sink, a drainer, an electric stove and a refrigerator between them, and enclosing the whole behind louvre doors.

As invariably happened, once we had done this for him, Mr Galliers Pratt decided to move. We followed him to his new house at 40 Belgrave Square, the top floor of which he then converted into a flat for his personal use. Later on, he took on a new director, who had three children, who were always running around the lower floors, and we were asked to affix bars at all the windows so that they wouldn't fall out. That wasn't the end of this client, however. He rang one day to say that the front of his house was in a rather bad state, which, indeed it was. The porch, in particular, was very dilapidated. The columns were crumbling away, and plaster was peeling off the cornices.

"What do you think, Mr Gilbert?" Mr Galliers Pratt said. "Dreadful, isn't it?"

"Well, yes," I agreed. I couldn't do otherwise.

"I should be delighted if you could be contracted to repair it," he said.

"What," I asked, "about the Grosvenor Estates' surveyor?" I knew they were the landlords of the property.

"I haven't seen him yet," he said.

"Oh, but you can't start work, you know, until he's contacted. He'll have to give his permission."

"You contact him, then," returned Mr Galliers Pratt, and walked off.

So I did, and eventually we were given permission to start work, and the Grosvenor Estates' surveyor supervised the job, and insisted that everything was replaced, stylistically, exactly as it had been originally. When they had finished, he went round and praised the workmen, and this pleased them immensely. It also pleased me, for, while many firms rely on advertisements to obtain more work, by far the most satisfying and economical way is to attract further clients by pleasing your existing ones, and especially their landlords! This way you get twice the number of recommendations.

Lady Lister of 101 Mount Street was recommended to us in this way.

"You have quite a reputation, Mr Gilbert," she said when I called on her. "I hear you always react favourably to unusual requests. Come with me."

She took me to a very large bedroom.

"Now," she said, "I want a fitted wardrobe built the whole length of this wall. I am tired of seeing Sir Percy's clothes all over the place."

So I got the men to put in a fitted wardrobe well over fifteen feet long, which so pleased Her Ladyship that she immediately wanted a little kitchen in her corridor, just as Mr Galliers Pratt had, and who, in fact, had recommended us in the first place. She in turn passed us on to a Mr Coit at 32 Hyde Park Gardens, who wanted his home refurbished throughout. It turned out to be a very big job, because he had two reception rooms, a dining room, a billiard room, six bedrooms and two bathrooms. Later, this was the house where Sir Winston Churchill wrote his memoirs, and eventually died.

With all these jobs coming in, the firm picked up well, and we were set fair for a new period of prosperity, but local authorities were beginning to loom large in our sort of work, and started to get in the way of commissions which we would have been pleased to accept. Sometimes, however, it worked the other way, as in the case of the Middle East Association which got in touch with us again because they had been told by the authorities that, owing to the increased use of their building, they had got to have an outside staircase fitted at the back. People often accuse local government offices of red tape – I have myself – and sometimes they are justified, but it is easy to ignore the fact that they have grave responsibilities, and must consider the welfare of the public at large. I have to confess that I have frequently found it difficult dealing with councils. In this particular case, they insisted on a steel staircase, and it had to be put in, expensive though it was.

It was no sooner finished than they found another problem. They condemned a four inch lead soil pipe, and its removal meant disturbing all the floors and walls in the house, as well as the shops below. The association's directors were very upset, but thought that, in view of their co-operation, the council would now, at last, agree to the removal of a chimney stack which served six chimneys. At first the council would not agree, and seemed set to refuse, despite several requests. This is the sort of attitude which gets them disliked, for the client feels they have gone more than halfway to meet the demand, but no such understanding is being reciprocated. So for a long time it was stalemate. Then, suddenly, one day they said the association could take the old stack down, provided the ornamental chimney at the top was left, as it was a unique feature of the building's character. So, we were allowed to remove the obsolete functional stack and to leave just one chimney – for aesthetic reasons! Such are the workings of local authorities.

We now started to spread out of London again, and, first of all, we went back to Hampstead, where we had worked so many years ago. This time we went to the home of Lord Chalfont, in Templewood Avenue. He was a very sociable man, and loved inviting large numbers of people to his parties. He also loved Hampstead, and did not want to move, but he found Templewood Avenue too small, despite the fact that his party room was twenty feet long by twenty feet wide. He wanted it made twenty feet longer still. We did this by extending the room a further twenty feet into the garden, and decorating the supports with fluted columns. The rest of the room was decorated in stippled cream, slightly wiped to give an antique effect. With such large numbers of influential people being invited to the house, and with the hope of further orders on our part, it was essential that we got it right, and got it right we did!

One of the most delightful and rewarding things about the clientele for whom we worked was their complete faith in us. Major Chamberlain wanted his mother's flat in Cadogan Gardens completely refurbished while she was away. He just gave us the keys and left us to it. It was always rather stressful when this happened, for you become responsible not only for the work in hand, but for the owner's furniture and fittings, and the safety of their valuables. Mrs Chamberlain, like Mrs Baird, had pictures. And in her case they weren't just valuable; some of them were priceless. It was a great worry. In the process of redecorating, many of them had to be taken down and stored, and we could not discuss anything with Mrs Chamberlain, as she was on a cruise. It gave me some sleepless nights, but needless to say, we eventually got the commission finished, and when Mrs Chamberlain returned some weeks later, she said she was well satisfied with the work and the care that had been taken of everything, including the pictures, which were now back in place.

As the Sixties drew to a close and the Seventies got under way, we acquired many other clients, and became a very large company. When this happens it is easy to lose contact with the individual clients, and to leave their idiosyncrasies to the foremen. But two clients touched my heart in a way that none of those who had gone before had ever done. I made them my special responsibility, and they made me ashamed of my earlier self-pity, when such a lot of trouble seemed to have come my way.

Two Fine Men

When I was a child I often heard my mother say that the sorrow in the world had to be spread around everyone, as one pair of shoulders could not support it. Going back to the bad winter when my father-in-law had come to live with us, I felt as if I were supporting all the trouble in the world myself. But later on, when I came to work for Mr Steibel and Mr Addinsell, and saw how they coped with their own personal misfortune, I recognised that they were an example for everyone else, including me.

In running a business you meet all types of people – the demanding, the undecided, the inconsistent, the impolite, the bullying, the snobbish – and every situation has to be assessed quickly, and the right response made. With Mr Steibel and Mr Addinsell I was at a loss; it's very difficult to summon up the right response to fortitude. Mr Steibel and Mr Addinsell had troubles so overwhelming that I was prepared to pardon them for being difficult, but, when they turned out to be two of the most accommodating gentlemen I had ever come across, it was very hard to deal with.

I first met Mr Victor Steibel in 1973. He was middle-aged, tall, impeccably dressed, and with that air of distinction that one found in a man at the top of his profession; in that profession he was famous as a dress designer, and numbered Princess Margaret, Princess Alexandra and Princess Alice among his clientele.

He had bought the lease of 17 Cavendish Square, W1, and here he had his rooms. He employed twenty-five seamstresses and ten other staff. We were originally called in because the weight of the sewing machines was so great that rolled steel joists bolted together had to be inserted into the floor. Furthermore, staff employed on highly specialised cutting and sewing were deemed to be in need of special lighting for the avoidance of glare and, to achieve this, we installed cove cornice lighting, which reflected up on to the ceiling and not on to the workers below.

After this, for years Victor Steibel called upon us for his decorating and maintenance work. And all the time I could see that his health was slowly deteriorating, until, the day came when he was forced to give up his business altogether. It was terrible for him, and I thought, then, that that would be the end of our connection with 17 Cavendish Square, but such was not the case. If anything, our contact with Mr Steibel increased, as he needed our help more and more. He was found to be suffering from multiple sclerosis, and his ability to move around became increasingly difficult. But his ill-health never impaired his good humour, or his interest in the world of fashion and design.

One day when I called to see him, he said, "Come in, Mr Gilbert. I hope you are well. Do sit down. Let us see what we can think up to make me mobile again! Not," he added, "that I want to be very mobile at the moment. I am writing my life story."

It was terribly sad to see him like this, sitting in an armchair, unable to move, covered in a blanket. He used to sit before the fire without moving for hours on end, and we used to discuss at great length all the improvements we could make to lessen his disability and make life easier for him. One idea we had was to drill through the vitriolite splashes round his bath and put in grab rails; we also fixed a long pole from floor to ceiling in the bathroom, so that he could hold on to it when he moved.

In the end, he had to be carried everywhere by his chauffeur, and it broke my heart to see him getting weaker and weaker, but still smiling.

It was through Mr Steibel that I met Richard Addinsell, the composer of the *Warsaw Concerto*, who originally lived in Launceston Place, although he spent a lot of his time in his house in Brighton.

Mr Addinsell was Mr Steibel's great friend, and I had often seen him when Kimber and James were decorating in Cavendish Square. At that time I little thought that one day we would be called upon by Mr Addinsell to do for him exactly what we had done for Mr Steibel when he had become ill. Over the years, the composer developed severe arthritis, so he sold his house in Launceston Place and bought a flat in Carlisle Mansions, in Cheyne Walk. Mr Steibel recommended us to him, and we were called in to prepare this new flat for occupation. It was in a very shabby state and had to be thoroughly cleaned and repainted. Kimber and James also made a large bookcase along one wall in the drawing room, and put cupboards underneath, specially designed to take his huge collection of records.

Tom Challis, the carpenter, was very nervous about these cupboards, or rather what to do with the hundreds and hundreds of gramophone records in the composer's collection.

"He wants his records sorted and put into the new cupboards," he confided to me. "What if I should break one?"

"Break one? Of course, you won't break one," I assured him.

"They're brittle," he retorted.

"I know they're brittle. All records are brittle. But they're not easily broken. You definitely won't break one," I told him, and, good man that he was, he didn't.

"There you are, Tom," I said to him so after afterwards. "What did I tell you? I said you wouldn't break a record, didn't I? And you didn't."

When the bookcase and cupboards were finished, and all the records had been sorted and put into their new home, we put castors on Mr Addinsell's chair so that he could push himself around. After that, we made a long table top to go the whole length of the bookcase, so that he could put his gramophone on it and play his 78s as and when the fancy took him, instead of having to wait for someone to get them out for him and set them on the record player.

As with Mr Steibel, we put grab rails round his bath and installed a chair to his size at the side of the bath. In the end he had to have a day, as well as a night nurse to help him, but, as long as Mr Steibel was alive, the chauffeur would first put Mr Steibel into the car and then come and get Mr Addinsell and put him in, too, and drive them both to Brighton for the weekend.

Although their vocations were in very different spheres, both men were artists, and united by the fact that they were both at the top of their professions, as well as by their cruel disablements, which, finally, left both of them absolutely bedridden.

I shall never forget these two men. When they were well, they put heart and soul into the work they had chosen to do, and, when they became ill and elderly, they still looked to extract from life all that life had to offer within the limitations imposed by their illnesses. Despite more than their share of trouble being loaded on to their shoulders, I never heard them complain. They were always cheerful and appreciative, but I often wondered how they felt in the night, so ill and unable to move.

I used to look at them and think what right had I had to inveigh against my own bad times?

Mr Addinsell was a great reader. He often told me he knew Kipling's 'If' by heart; he was, it was obvious, resolved to live by it, especially the lines:

> ...force your heart, and nerve, and sinew
> To serve your turn long after they have gone,
> And so hold on when there is nothing in you,
> Except the will which says to them – Hold on.

These were the words which Mr Addinsell, and Mr Steibel, too, exemplified more than anyone else I ever met. They were *two fine men, two very fine men*, indeed.

Chapter Thirteen

Starting Over

"The old order changeth," so said Tennyson and it's only when you get older that you realise how things have changed. That sounds obvious. But whilst the big changes that hit you can been seen as turning points in life, it is with surprise that you suddenly notice how all those unremarked imperceptible alterations have added up, in the end, to a way of life quite unconnected with earlier years. When I look back, I can hardly believe what has happened to the world since I was a lad.

And coming in between the bombshell changes and the little ones you don't notice, are those you know are coming. One of these for me was that the time for the expiry of the lease of our premises at George Street was getting nearer. At first it could be put out of the mind, then it loomed up more regularly, and finally the day came when *something had to be done*. Kimber and James was going to have to move, for the new rents being set were out of the question. To move, especially for a medium-sized business, is worrying, for one of the secrets of success is continuity; the stabilising effect of having a fixed, central head office which clients get to know, and which demonstrates a continuing family interest in the firm, gives customers a feeling of security, and this ensures prosperity.

What we decided to do to minimise the impact of the upheaval and reduce overheads, was to move the office into our works at Bentinck Mews. It was near Baker Street, and not all that far from George Street, where people had been used to coming. So we went ahead and converted part of the works area and supplies depot into offices. When we had finished, Bentinck Mews had a storage unit in the basement, a garage, new ladies' and gents' toilets, a paint shop – and offices! It shows what can be done with a bit of ingenuity. And it is still all in place today!

But at the same time, while congratulating ourselves on our transfer and refurbishment, it was sad for my brother and me, who had devoted a lifetime to its success, to see the firm seemingly without anyone to take over when we had to retire. In some cases, a firm placed in this position may even have to close down, if it cannot dispose of its goodwill, especially if that goodwill largely depends on the relationship between practitioner and client, as ours did. But in this we were lucky. It was with delight that we saw a new star rising (not in the east as in the Nativity story, but in the south from Kent) in the shape of my nephew, David. Just as we were all privately wondering what would become of Kimber and James in the next decade or so, the company David was working for started experiencing difficulties, and thus it was he asked if he could come and work for us. He was promptly taken on, and did so well that today he is head of the firm, managing our business, in which integrity, efficiency and just dealing are considered the norm. He has a son who, hopefully, may one day follow his father, just as his father followed his uncles; so for the foreseeable future Kimber and James seems secure.

At the time of our move, however, I was rather apprehensive. For one thing, Peter Jones, which had always been a great source of revenue to us, decided to close down their decoration department. At the same time, many of our best skilled and loyal workmen died or retired. Dear old Jim Hoe was one that died, and Miss Spanier of Peter Jones retired completely, after carrying on alone for a while. It was hard to replace such people. Well, it's true to say, they are never replaced. For each new generation brings with it different standards, and, of course, what I considered acceptable in my day was not considered acceptable in the 1970s. Men were different. Paint was different. Clients were different. Contacts were different. You just had to adapt as best you could.

Even more unsettling was that the country, likewise, seemed different. Things had turned – or so it appeared to me – upside down. For example, prices were going up and up, and with them, wages. Most of the time we managed to keep things on an even keel, and, by and large, the men were satisfied. But I remember we had one painter who said he wanted 3d an hour over the painter's rate, because he was required to mix paint. This was, admittedly, a skilled job, but money would not stretch to such lengths at that point. As he would not carry out his duties as foreman, I took away the 3d an hour, and the man complained to his union. A union representative came to the site to examine the complaint and about a week later I received a letter from the union to demand that the man's rights be respected. However, when I think I am in the right, as I am sure I have already told you, I will not give way to opposition demands. Therefore, I sent a letter to the union to say that their representative was wrong to visit my property without my permission. He was trespassing. I heard no more from the union, and soon afterwards the painter resigned. We were glad to see him go – when times are hard, you cannot afford such people.

It all comes as a shock though. I mean things like being challenged by a union, especially when one is doing one's best to keep things going and men in employment. I reacted, as I have described, and always have reacted, but inside I felt troubled and alone. Brother Tom had been taken ill, was no longer able to come to the office on three mornings a week as he had been doing, and his Harley Street specialist said he would never work again, which he didn't. All decisions were mine, and I continued for most of the 70s, until I eventually reduced my workload by going to the office part-time. But I never gave up.

However, one day in the early 1980s I was in the library changing my wife's library books when something that I had never experienced before happened to me. I collapsed. One minute I was reaching up to a shelf for a book, and the next I found myself sitting on a seat in the street with an ambulance man standing over me. At first I thought it was something to do with my shoulder, for which I had been having treatment. I had been told by the specialist, whom I had consulted, that it was rheumatism, and various remedies had been prescribed for it. But in the end I got it better myself by wrapping an electric blanket round it. That did it. No more rheumatism for me, I thought. However, when I came round and was sufficiently recovered, I reckoned that my passing out must have been owing to the fact that I had been reaching up for a book, and twisted my arm, as that was the last thing I remembered.

The ambulance man insisted he must take me to hospital, but I was having none of it. I was equally insistent that I was going home, and, what was more, driving myself there, which I did. But I was severely cautioned, and taken to task for this attitude by the ambulance crew, who told me not only was it inadvisable, but that I would be a danger to other road users, and, looking back on it now, I admit that they were right. At the time, I had just one thought. I must get home to Millie. I told no one about the incident, except the doctor when he came visiting; he said I had collapsed from strain.

For Millie was bedridden, and had been for several months. She had been to hospital after hospital, and in the end she was taken into the Royal Masonic Hospital, where she died. We had been married for forty-nine years, and the day she died was the worst day of my whole life. I was absolutely devastated. I didn't know what to do. Before, when something awful had happened, I had tried to cope with it. Not perhaps exactly, or as bravely, as I would afterwards have wished. But I tried, I honestly did. Now I lost the will.

So, I sat down and thought about what I was going to do. I had to do something, and I had to do it quickly.

I decided I would go back to work full-time. Although I was by now eighty-two, and very tired from the years of strain of nursing, as well as going to the office and supervising jobs quite alone, now that I no longer had brother Tom or Merry to help me. But I decided, quite deliberately, to go back to work full-time. After a month or so, I bought a season ticket for the football. It was lonely there, too, without Victor, who had moved out of London. But it was football. That meant that with a full week's work, and Saturdays accounted for, only Sundays were unoccupied. I suddenly had an inspiration: bowls! Hadn't I always wanted to play bowls? To start off with I joined the bowls section of the local Woodside Park Club where I was received with open arms as the membership was only about twelve members. The bowling green was in a very poor state, and open to all elements of the weather and dogs, etc. With assistance I was able to fix a wire fence around the bowling green with wooden gates at the entrance. After two years I was made captain and our membership rose to about forty players. I then thought that it was time for a younger man to take over.

The club's bar lounge was in a very poor state so a scheme of decorations was proposed and approved and carried out by the members whom I assisted. Also we decorated the ladies' and gents' cloakrooms and then the exterior of the building for which I supplied sixty gallons of paint at cost price. We then finished by decorating the main concert hall. Meanwhile, I was introduced to the Mansfield Bowls Club and then to the London Masonic Bowls Association.

When the Glebelands (Finchley) Indoor Bowls was formed in 1990 I, living locally, joined as a 'founder member', and resigned from the Mansfield.

I have now played in several matches for the London Masonic at Southampton, Worthing, Crawley, Bournemouth etc., etc. When playing at Southampton, which is one of the oldest greens in England, we were told this was the green that King Charles II played on. In those days they played with wooden bowls with no bias, and the captain for the year was called 'sir'.

So, as far as bowls goes, I can thoroughly recommend it – for anyone who has suffered a terrible blow in life, for the game itself, for the gentle exercise it provides, and for the people you meet, all of whom I have found to be sociable and more than willing to explain the game to you when you begin. So never be put off. Take it up! Right away! Today! That's my advice, for I myself am eternally grateful to the game of bowls.

About this time, too, my own Masonic Lodge was rapidly losing all its members, so we that were left amalgamated with a South African Lodge, which was resident in London, and here begins another chapter in my life. I found myself among all these coloured gentlemen, and very nice they were to me. I turned out to be the Lodge's oldest member and I got to be selected for the Senior London Grand Chapter rank, the highest honour given for services rendered on behalf of the Masons, except the Supreme Grand Chapter rank. It was very gratifying, I can tell you, not only to be welcomed in by all these younger people, but to be honoured, too.

So, now, things were really beginning to perk up, and I looked around to see what else I could do, and being of an optimistic nature, I undertook several measures to get myself back into trim. I started to do my daily exercises again. I started to look at my diet, and I have ever since begun the day with half a pint of milk and a banana. It is excellent for stamina, and another thing that I can recommend. I did think of retiring, or at least going part-time, so that I would have more time for my leisure activities, but it could not be done, as I was assisting with a very big job in Grosvenor Square. However, I did not let that stop me from exploring other avenues in the time I did get off.

One of these was to renew my enthusiasm for travelling. I went round all my friends and relatives; those who were some way away, such as Sweden, and a bit too far to go, came to see me instead.

Then, when that was all done, I joined the National Trust and went on all their visits. This turned out to be of great interest, not least as the tours often took in places where the firm had had commissions, and, apart from Lady Isobel, whom I have mentioned earlier, I also met up with Lord Hartford at Ragley Hall, and Lady Price at Wakehurst. It is a fine feeling to go round with a group of people, and while they are making admiring comments, silently think, "I put that cornice up there" or "I rebuilt that fireplace"; the pride of the craftsman comes out very strongly in such circumstances, and you feel you have left a little bit of yourself for posterity.

In looking for places to visit, one of my great joys was to rediscover Dulwich. I went back not only to reminisce and to look at the old house in Crystal Palace Road, and Heber Road School, and the archway in Oglander Road, where the cows used to amble through into their field, but also to look up the history of the place, and to appreciate all those things I had never bothered my head with when I was a youngster, larking about with Stan White, and knowing absolutely nothing of all the Gainsboroughs and Rubens and Murillos and Van Dycks in the Picture Gallery. I don't suppose I could have even told you that there was a picture gallery, let alone that it was well known, and held what had once been intended as the nucleus of the National Gallery. I have now rectified all that.

First of all, I looked up where the name of Dulwich came from, and discovered that it could perhaps be traced to De la Wyk, a man who had had land in Camberwell about 1100 in the reign of Henry I. Then it had changed alternatively to Dilwisshe, Dullidg, Duliage and Dilwik, until it finally took the form of Dulwich, which we have today. The manor of Dulwich used to belong to the Priory of Bermondsey, presented to them by this same King Henry around 1127, and they held it for about four hundred years. Around 1544 Henry VIII sold the Manor to a Thomas Galton Goldsmith and it was his heirs who sold it to the actor, Edward Alleyn, whom everyone associates with the district, because of Dulwich College.

Edward Alleyn and the chalybeate waters were both well known in Dulwich in the seventeenth century. Alleyn obtained the right to the Manor in 1606 and by 1607 was buying up other parts of the district, namely, three tenements and twenty-two acres. It was this actor, Shakespeare's contemporary, who set up the Foundation that was the origin of Dulwich College, the public school which still stands today.

The original college was opened in 1619 and was called the 'College of God's Gift'. It consisted of four fellows, who were the preacher, the master, the usher and the organist, and thirty poor pensioners, who were twelve poor scholars, six poor old brothers, six poor sisters, and six chaunters in the choir to teach music. Alleyn left a lot of rules and regulations regarding the running of his Foundation, including the fact that only people with the name of 'Alleyn' should have the master's or warden's position. He also stipulated that the inmates were to have beer at breakfast and in the evening, and that their coats were to be of good cloth, lined, and of a sombre colour. The college has changed many times since the first one, and there is now also a girl's school, set up by James Alleyn, who was a warden in 1712. There was also another famous school in the district, famous because of its famous pupil, Byron, and this was Dr Glennie's Academy. However, I never knew of it; all I knew was that I thought I should have been allowed into the 'proper' school, instead of being sent to Heber Road.

I also found out that Dulwich and the surrounding districts were quite well known for their chalybeate wells, the water of which, as long ago as 1678, was being sold, not only in Dulwich, but in London. In this time of cures, taking the water was said to remedy all manner of ailments; this particular sulphurous water was highly prized, no doubt because the worse the taste the better it was thought to be for you. There were several wells in the vicinity, and the one belonging to Dulwich was close by the Green Man.

Today, Dulwich still retains its village atmosphere, with its leafy roads, and cricket pitch and the park, which was the gift of the college. It was here that I, well shielded by the trees which had once been part of Dulwich Wood, used to climb over the back fence of the houses bordering the park to scrump apples. On the south side of this wood the gypsies had had their encampment, and it was said that Margaret Finch, their queen, lived in a house on Gipsy Hill. It all sounds romantic and dreamlike, and it is a shame that the wood, like the original Dulwich Common, has disappeared. Nobody would think, looking at it now, that only a hundred years ago Croxted Road was a crooked (as the name implies) winding lane. But there you go – that's progress. My pond at the cross-roads, where I used to go fishing with Stan White, is still there, though, and as long as that remains, I can allow myself the luxury of thinking that Dulwich is safe and that I have not yet been cut off from my childhood.

Not that I am sentimental about it. I have been doing things which I couldn't have done had I remained imprisoned in my youth. For example, I have been to the Festival Hall to hear the son of my Swedish friends playing the cello, and hired a box at the Royal Albert Hall for ten of my London friends. I have taken up bridge and been to a bowling alley. Last but not least, I have started to fly abroad. I had never flown before, but there has to be a first time for everything. So I flew off to Spain and to Jersey, and I will still fly when the mood takes me.

Now, all of these occupations have been great fun, and I often reflect how lucky I have been to make the comeback; I know it's harder for men to adapt, for they have all the cooking and shopping and cleaning and washing and gardening to do, as well as trying to find distractions, and some of these things do not come easily to them. But if I can do it, so can everyone else. Never despair. Of course, I had good friends, especially my lovely niece, Linda, who often used to come after being on duty all night as a nursing sister at one of the big London hospitals. I also had my two good lady neighbours next door.

Thus it was that I got back to normal, and around the middle of the Eighties I eventually did get to the point of going only part-time to the office. That is to say, I went in two days a week, and covered for all holidays and, in addition, on big jobs.

Really, I was quite contented, and thought it would go on for ever.

But, as I said at the beginning, everything changes, as you will see. It's just that it's not in the way you expect it to be.

Chapter Fourteen
Football all the Way

I have been trying to think of something that spans my century, something that was there at the beginning and is still there now. And I make no apology for saying that the only thing I can think of, as far as the ordinary man goes, is football. Nationally the century is divided up by crises that come and go, as do the monarchs, the prime ministers and the leading figures. The same with private lives, with their great sorrows and great happinesses. But football is like Tennyson's 'Brook'; it goes on, and just as it was there in 1900, so it is there at the end of the century: changed, but there.

You cannot say that of many other things. They may claim the same tenure, things, such as art, or music, or blood sports. But I am talking about a movement, a phenomenon really, that touches a great part of the working population. I can't say it is the only sport followed by the working man, for there are other sports, coursing, for example, that he follows. But not world-wide, and certainly not as innocent as football, which has the great advantage of confining its bloody encounters to human beings who want to play it, and those who want to watch it. It is the great escape.

Football pays homage to many things – skill, courage, commercialism – but, above all, its worshippers flock to the shrine of escapism, and in my case this was situated in Selhurst Park. There, there was indeed a palace at whose gates I could stand and worship. Not Buckingham Palace, the Élysée Palace, the Palace Cinema, or any other palace; not even the Crystal Palace itself, after which my club was named, and which I knew very well as it was just up the road; we called it The Glasshouse. That palace was one of the wonders of the nineteenth century, fashioned in glass, hundreds of feet long, and full of artefacts said to be boosting Great Britain's trade. (In vain was I told that these self same objects which had been on view close to home, had been transferred to the Victoria and Albert Museum.) Truth to tell, the only fact I could remember was that the original Crystal Palace had been plagued by sparrows, and when Queen Victoria complained about them to the Duke of Wellington, he merely replied, "Sparrowhawks, ma'am." I could always remember the sparrowhawks, but not much else except the night it burnt down and its flames lit up half of London.

It was exciting, but not half as exciting as that other palace, which was nicknamed 'The Glaziers'.

Few people who follow football are aware of the humble origins of some of the great clubs of the present day. The oldest Football League club, Notts County, started about one hundred and fifty years ago as St James's Church Club, and Arsenal, fifty years later was the team drawn from men working at the munitions depot in Woolwich, South London, which explains why to this day they are nicknamed 'The Gunners'. My own team was formed in 1851, when a number of workmen who were maintaining the original Crystal Palace when it was situated in Hyde Park, decided to form a works team. It was 1906 when the team became full-time and professional, playing on Sydenham Hill where the Crystal Palace construction, pane by pane, had been resited after Prince Albert's Great Exhibition was over. And, incidentally, that was where the Cup Final was played until Wembley Stadium in North London was built. And that's where for me it all began.

This was before the game took off as a commercial enterprise, and the glamour days had yet to come. Extraneous hype was provided for us by the local town band who mustered in the middle of the pitch and played marches or Gilbert and Sullivan before the match. Much later, the majorettes made their appearance; but whatever was going on, everyone enjoyed it. Crowds were larger then than they are today, and their roar could be heard almost as far away as the district boundary, so even if we were late we could tell how our team was doing.

It was euphoric just to approach the ground, joining everyone else, all going the same way. We went through turnstiles – little open ones – to get in, and it cost about sixpence or eightpence in 1912 (1/40th of a pound sterling) to about one and sixpence (1/14th of a pound) in 1945. Today, prices range from £8 to £20 or more. A man has to think now before digging deep into his pocket to treat another member of his family or a friend to a game.

Ben Bateman, in 1922 Crystal Palace kit, playing at the 'nest'.

It was my brother, Victor, who treated me when he first started work.

"As soon as I earn some money, I will take you to a professional football match," he promised, and he was as good as his word.

I was ten years old at the time, and just getting there was exciting for me. First we walked to Lordship Lane Station, and went by train to the huge, long Crystal Palace Station. Then we walked across Crystal Palace Parade, and down Annerley Hill to the football ground behind The Glasshouse. I hopped and skipped. I ran on ahead and then ran back. I could hardly contain myself. And, for all that, I don't remember much about that first match, except that it made a deep impression on me and I so enjoyed myself that I became a Crystal Palace supporter overnight and have been ever since.

I remember it cost sixpence to sit on the grass, and that I was all polished up, squeaky clean and shining to do just that. I was very proud of myself, for in 1912 football was acknowledged to be a man's game. It was the day father got away from the wife and the kids. It was his one half-day of leisure, for in 1912 he had probably been working all the morning before he got to the game. Sunday was home day, unless he was one of those who went to the pub and then came home drunk and pulled the tablecloth and dinner off the table just to show who was boss. But at the football he didn't have to prove anything. It was a masculine place. You hardly ever saw a woman in the ground. It was here, after a week of drudgery, a man, whether a good husband and father, or a bad one, could let off steam; he could shout, abuse the referee, and swear. And I, John William Humphrey Gilbert, all four feet of me, was being allowed into this world. Initiated, you might say. It signified my transition, I thought, from child to adult. Of course, it didn't really, but I felt it did. And so I was anxious to return. I couldn't wait for Saturday fortnight. But I don't think I often went on the anticipated day. My elder brother probably couldn't afford it. My enthusiasm wasn't affected, however. I could always stand outside and listen to the crowd, and hope – invariably in vain – that a soft hearted doorman, like the one down at the Dulwich Hamlet ground, would let me in at half-time.

In 1914, when war broke out, the Admiralty requisitioned the whole of the Crystal Palace grounds and the football team was turned out; therefore it transferred itself to the Herne Hill running track for the time being. The teams in those days became very mixed, and any player who was on leave from the Services was asked to play. After the war the club moved on to The Nest, a ground which belonged to Croydon Common FC, and which they had vacated. The names I call to mind from those days are, above all, Feebury, McCracken, Strong and Bateman. I know the football was made of leather and quite heavy; heading it could give you a headache if you didn't have the know-how. The golden rule was always to have both feet off the ground at the moment when your head made contact with the ball; that way no harm was done. It was a skill you had to learn quickly, for the seasons could be wet and the ground soggy and very muddy. The ball often got stuck in the mud, and the players, if they were charged or slipped, came up covered in mud and looked a sorry sight.

The ground then had only a small stand with seats for two hundred people. There were sloping sides all round leading down to the pitch, and these slopes had iron barricades to stop the spectators from sliding down on top of each other when they leaned forward. As time went on steps were cut into the ground and this was a great help. At a later stage these were formed in concrete, which was an even greater help.

My enthusiasm never flagged. As soon as I could earn a few pennies I would save them up to go by myself, if no one could, or would, take me. I sat on the grass as near as possible to the touch line, sucking my gobstoppers, and memorising the name of every player on the field. I can see them now: Stan Charlton, George Smith, Albert Harry, Peter Simpson, Billy Callender, and later Fred and Albert Dawes, Dave Bassett, Ronnie Rooke, George Graham, and countless other players who, apart from their footballing ability, had other qualities I shall never forget. One such was Phil Bates, who played centre-half with only one arm and was never off-balance. Then there was Jack Alderson, the goalkeeper, whom we used to call 'The Flying Angel'. He was a great hero because of his feat in saving all the shots at goal during a cup-tie match. Although the Palace was leading one-nil they were hopelessly outplayed, but because of Alderson we won.

Come to think of it, goalkeepers are a race apart. Remember Jackson? He was an expert in Latin and Greek. And Burridge? He turned somersaults in front of goal. And Glazier who always reminded us that the Palace were called 'The Glaziers'? Goalies in the days before Jackson and Burridge came on the scene wore the stock-in-trade kit of goalkeepers everywhere – an ordinary cap, a thick green jersey and black shorts. The other ten players in the team wore heavy,

149

coloured shirts without numbers, and shorts that could be described as long shorts or 'short longs' which came below the knee. It wasn't considered decent for a soccer player to show his knees.

The game was much slower and less scientific than it is today, with five forwards, three mid-field men, two full backs and a goalkeeper as the norm. It was also less dangerous. For one thing, spectators didn't throw things. And, if one of the players did get carried off injured, there was no substitute to take his place. The team merely continued with ten men, which is always a good psychological boost to the crowd. It introduces an element of one side's having less than a sporting chance.

Also, there was no 'star' system, though, of course, we all had our own favourites and convictions as to whom was going to come out on top of the score sheet. Best of all, the players were in it for love of the game, for they were so poorly paid that it is correct to say that most of the spectators earned as much, if not more, than those on the field.

And so it went on. All over the country. In my case, as far as Crystal Palace were concerned, they, like most other clubs, had a chequered career. Over the years they 'went up', they 'went down', and eventually they achieved a place in the Premiership League. And, given coverage by the media, a new sort of 'star' arrived – the Matt Busbys, the Don Revies, the Brian Cloughs; at Selhurst Park, this was Malcolm Allison, who was set apart from all other managers by his fedora and extrovert personality. He had such charisma that whether the team was winning or losing, he made you feel your team was important; in fact, the only team worth following. He should never have gone. Nor should Stevie Coppell after him. I shall never forget when we 'went up' when Coppell was in charge, and the fans all crowded on to the pitch in front of the directors' box and chanted:

"Stevie Coppell's Red Army! Stevie Coppell's Red Army!"
"We want Coppell! We want Coppell!"

These things make football. As do the show-biz people I have spotted in among the spectators. For example, of later years I've seen Ronnie Corbett and Ronnie Barker, David Jensen and Angus Deayton. Not forgetting Windsor Davies. I walked along with him once as we left the ground, and he was signing autographs all the time we made our way through the crowd.

"It must get very tiring, having to do that wherever you go," I said to him.

"I tell you, boyo," he laughed. "It's when they stop asking you for your autograph that you begin to worry. And that's more tiring."

Over the years, football has ceased to be what it was when I went to that first match at ten years old. Now it has a social agenda. We have restaurants, lounges, TVs, tannoy, sponsorship, electronic information, disability access, family sections, shops and marketing departments. It is now football in the community, but it is more true to say that football has embraced the community, rather than the community embracing it as it used to.

At the Palace all these activities can be enjoyed in the knowledge that the Palace is relatively safe, because crowd trouble, I mean real trouble, is hardly ever encountered there. Generally speaking, you can approach the ground on a Saturday afternoon unworried about violence. However, I do remember one Crystal Palace–Birmingham City game in 1989 when there was crowd invasion of the pitch. I must say the sight of a dozen or so officers from the Metropolitan Mounted Police galloping diagonally across the pitch to repel the invaders was a sight worth seeing. For one wicked moment, I was reliving the Charge of the Light Brigade, and it was for real, not on film. It's a pity, I think, that the police horses nowadays have to wear protective tack. It spoils the look of them, keeps in mind the violent times in which we live, and reduces Palace's excellent non-violent record among the spectators to that of other unruly clubs.

Because of this problem in football, and to comply with the Taylor Report, the ground had to become all-seating, and the last grassy bank on which we fans used to stand has disappeared. It all looks very smart now, but I hanker after a link with the old days, when we were 'The Glaziers', not the 'Eagles' as we are known today, and when, unbelievably, Edward VII was on the throne, and I was on the touchline. Oh, happy days!

Chapter Fifteen
Clamped!

It was Regent's Park. And high summer. The west side of the Outer Circle Road was quiet, for the noise of the traffic from Park Road, which ran parallel, did not penetrate the gardens and trees, and, in any case, just before eleven o'clock it was falling off. It was the best time of day. As yet hardly anyone about, except for the few cars that were arriving early to take advantage of the free parking which was allowed from 11 a.m. to midnight. Parking had become a great problem in the West End, Chelsea and Fulham where most of our jobs were. This was especially so when carrying materials to the sites; we used to park on yellow lines and hope there wouldn't be a ticket when we got back. It was also expensive: £1.00 an hour. So, whenever possible when going to the office, I parked in Regent's Park to save the expense, which could add up to a lot over a week.

And the day I am talking about was no exception. I drove from Finchley, got out of my car, looked around, and felt quite pleased with life. I liked London. To the south of where I stood was Baker Street; a few drivers had already parked and left to walk to the station to go into town. To the north was Lord's. I loved to spend a day there watching the cricket. And this was where the majority of the men who were now standing by their cars would be heading. It was all a leisurely business. We didn't bother to speak. Most of us just leant on the side of our car roofs, waiting for the magical moment when we could safely leave our vehicles and be off. I remember looking across the park. It was almost deserted, except for a few mothers pushing prams or playing with small children. On the path close by there were pensioners exercising their dogs. And a workman or two. But at this time of day no one else. No office workers eating sandwiches, no commuters reading the paper, no lovers, no schoolchildren. Just grass, and emptiness, and the dappled pattern of leaves on the road surface and the cars – and there weren't many of those before eleven.

The men going northwards to Lord's started to amble off. I wished I were going with them, but I wasn't. Today was one of my working days. About five to eleven, I locked the car, put on my jacket, collected all my papers and, after making sure everything was in order, began the mile walk to Bentinck Mews to start my day's work. All day I assisted in supervising jobs, taking telephone calls, settling disputes among the workmen, giving them instructions for the next day, checking accounts, and at five o'clock I got ready to go home. I was eighty-six. I reckoned I deserved it.

I walked back very slowly. The London streets were airless. I thought how glad I should be to get into the cool of the park, and sit down for a few minutes' relaxation before starting the drive home in the rush hour, so I entered the leafy green environs with a sigh.

And then I saw it. Bright yellow. I had been clamped.

In the less than five minutes between leaving the car and eleven o'clock a traffic warden had come and clamped me. On the windscreen was a note to say I must go to Marble Arch car pound and pay a fine before I could be unclamped. So, I had to walk to Baker Street and take the bus to Marble Arch, and then from there walk to the car pound – after I had found out where it was. There I had to pay £45 and was told to return to my vehicle and wait for about two hours, after which time an official would come and unclamp the wheel.

I walked back to the bus, and then from Baker Street back to my car, and I was very, very tired. I also felt rather resentful. All this for parking perhaps only one or two minutes before time. And it wasn't as if the road had been full. It wasn't. There was plenty of room for everyone who wanted to park there.

I undid the car door, got in and sat down. I was very glad to sit down. But I didn't just sit. I thought. And what I thought was that I had been treated rather meanly. If this is what they were going to do to me, then I wouldn't play ball. I wouldn't go to work. No more income tax for a start going into the Exchequer's coffers. Occasionally the citizen can hit back. And I did. I had been made angry. So, from that moment on, for me – retirement, especially as my nephew had taken over the running of the business and there was nothing for me to worry about.

It was quite a nice feeling. Never again would I have to sit waiting for traffic officials to make my car available to me to drive home. They came about seven o'clock, and I got home at eight, which, anyone will agree, was too long a day for a man of my age.

For a couple of days I thought I would give up driving altogether. That way I'd have no more hassle. Then I thought, 'Why should I? Why should I let some petty-minded official get me down? Certainly not!' But once the idea of turning in the car had come into my head I found it hard to dislodge. "But why dislodge it?" I reasoned. "Why not simply exchange this car for another? That way I shall be turning it in and getting my own back on the 'job's worth' brigade." One should never be defeated by this sort of thing.

So, on the Saturday morning following, I went to a Hadley Highstone garage in my old car, and came out the owner of another. A brand new Peugeot. That, I reckoned, was the way to stand up to officialdom.

And it paid off. I can recommend it. By the following year I did not know how I had ever found time to go to work. I took on new duties as a steward at the Glebelands Bowling Club, and with more time to spare I could now undertake more matches, and what was even better, put myself up for selection in many more away games. I also decided to have the house completely redecorated, and as I had to be away competing, I had to give my house keys to a workman, just as years before keys had been given to me.

After a while, I decided to sever all my ties with work, except Kimber and James, and so I sold all my other shares in subsidiary companies. With that done, the house re-painted, and a new car, I could, for the first time in my life, now devote myself entirely to leisure.

And very nice it was, too.

Reflections

Once I had retired, I started to think. Not much, but a little bit. The first thought that came into my head was that this was the first occasion I had, indeed, had time to think. After that, I considered it would be a good idea to have some perspectives on my life, and these

I found fell into three categories. They were: regret, gratitude, and amazement.

To begin with I considered my education, and realised what a great regret it was to me that I had not had a better one. I started Heber Road School at seven and left at fourteen, and it was simply a council school. Even so, at fourteen, I was not ready to leave, but my family were poor. We learnt to go without the better things in life without question. Even education. And because I had been brought up in the shadow of Dulwich College, I could not help thinking what a difference it would have made if I had been on the inside of that Dulwich College fencing looking out, instead of the small boy I had been, looking in. Not that I regarded the college boys in their whites with envy. I had no conception of that. Nor do I envy them now, looking back. It's just that... supposing... Dulwich College... what couldn't I have done?

Well, for a start I might have turned Kimber and James into another Higgs and Hill, or a McAlpine's. I would have had the knowledge and the confidence, to go all out, actively, for expansion. Today the firm might have been a household name. And, I could have had such conversations with the clients. I might have discussed naval tactics with Lord Mountbatten, or the technique of great actors such as Henry Irving with Laurence Olivier, or poetry and drama with Sir John Gielgud. It is not beyond possibility, for I always found that the really top notch people were more than willing to share information and talk. It is only the mediocre who treat workmen as workmen.

After education, my next even bigger regret was that I had not been better able to help my mother, who was so kind and lovely, and who worked so hard, and was often in pain but never complained. I think particularly of the medicine that might have eased her pain, but which we couldn't buy; I think, too, of the little treats, simple, tiny things, like a bunch of violets, or a box of chocolates, which weren't affordable, and which are now so easy to come by, but then were not to be contemplated. Ah, sugared almonds! Now I remember, that's what she would have liked. I wish I could see the look in her grey eyes if I had been able to come through the door with a box of sugared almonds tied in pink ribbon, the kind you buy in French pâtisseries. The same wish goes for my sisters. If only we had had enough money for them to have stayed at home and not be sent away into service the moment they were fourteen. "Put your feet under someone else's table" used to be the saying at that time, and my sisters were no different from anyone else. They were at school one day wearing their gym slips, and the next they were dressed by their employers in a cap and apron, learning to be parlour maids. They were lucky to find positions, we thought at the time. So, tears or no tears, they had to go.

But perhaps my greatest regret, and the one that comes back to me most often, is the loss of my father, killed as the war was ending, whom I knew only from the times when he came home on leave. He was cruelly snatched away from me, just as I was getting to know him. It is the only regret I have that is tinged with bitterness, for he had more than served his country. Did not his country ask too much of him and all the others like him? Looking back, I think it did.

So those are my regrets. What about my gratitude?

First of all, I realise what a lot I owe to Mr Whiteman, my teacher, and how I wish that he were still alive today so that I could search him out and tell him how much I owe him. What education I did manage to achieve at Heber Road is thanks to him, and I shall always remember him with affection. And I can still get by on what he taught me. I can still add up at the check-out in the supermarket quicker than the girl with the calculator. What do modern day educational methods have to say to that?

After Mr Whiteman, my gratitude goes to my brother, Tom. I admired him greatly when I was growing up. I used to look up to him, and go to him for advice, and I don't remember that he ever let me down. I also remember that he was not my full brother, but my step-brother, so he might even have had cause to have been jealous of me and my mother's new husband. But he never was, and that's a wonderful characteristic to possess. In return I had absolute faith in him, and he must have had faith in me, for he took me into the firm, as I've described. In that way he became not only my brother, and friend, but my employer too; and eventually, of course, we became partners. I hope I fulfilled his trust in me. I think I did. I tried to, anyhow. There are lots and lots of other people to whom I am grateful, especially my niece, Linda, and my next door neighbours; in fact, everyone who helped me when my wife was so ill. Such people restore one's faith in human nature, and I am glad I have reflected in this direction, for one should never forget kindness or let it grow dim.

Finally, I reflected on what had happened to the world during my life's span. This is where the amazement comes in. I was born only the year after Queen Victoria died, and after her I have lived through five other reigns. What changes I have witnessed! They would fill a book on their own. I have gone from lighting the fire under the copper to boil the clothes to washing machines, from lamps and candles to electric light, from the bustle to the mini skirt. And everybody's life has been changed by the speed of travel. When I was a lad it took weeks to sail to Australia, now it takes a mere twelve hours to fly there. Even more dramatic have been world affairs. Great wars have taken place in my lifetime, but who would dare go to war today, now that nuclear bombs make annihilation possible? There would be no country left to conquer. I suppose that is one of the biggest changes. The arms manufacturer can't sit at home any longer watching his profit mount by supplying arms to far away armies; he is in as much danger as everyone else.

So what I see today is not governments under pressure to make territorial claims, or pursue an ideology, but forever trying to fulfil the demands for greater and greater welfare and social services. Can you imagine putting barefooted children before conquering the colonies in Edwardian days? Now only small wars are allowed – small wars and state welfare. But even that does not stop the suffering. I look back with amazement at what has been achieved, but I also look with amazement at the suffering that still goes on.

These are my reflections. They come and go like waves on the sea shore, and sometimes other smaller reflections like the colour of Millie's hair, or the day I earned my first sovereign – wavelets you might call them – are interspersed with my big three: regret, gratitude and amazement.

Bowling Along

I have to tell you that my geraniums have been particularly good this year, and I trust they will be next year. My geraniums, though I haven't mentioned them before, are a measure of my success. My secret success, that is, the success I carry around with me inside my head. And I like to succeed. When I was very young I made up my mind that I would not always be poor, and in order to achieve this aim

I knew I would have to be successful. But this state of affairs is elusive. It does not come by wishing. You require luck, and graft, and persistence – just the qualities I have to bring to my geraniums. So I am pleased they are doing well, and in return they provide me with an abundance of colourful blooms all the year round – summer *and winter*. Gardening has always been a part of my life. I love it. It started during the First World War when food was in short supply – rationed – and vegetables, especially potatoes, were almost impossible to obtain. We were so fed up with artichokes or swedes, which were all the greengrocer could supply, that when I was told that most people who could do so were growing their own potatoes, I decided to go ahead and grow ours.

I was only fourteen at the time and very tired from my work at the munitions factory. However, I eyed the patch of ground some twelve by fifteen feet outside the kitchen window of 251 Crystal Palace Road and thought: 'Potatoes!' However it was not as easy as I had imagined. It was jolly hard work to get the ground dug up and prepared. But when it was done, it was quite exciting to plant the seed potatoes (supervised by my mother), and when they actually started pushing up I was very pleased with myself. I took a lot of time watching them and earthing them to make channels between the rows so that when I watered them the water would get through to the roots. This is what I had been told had to be done, so I did it, and was rewarded in my first agricultural experiment with an abundance of potatoes.

I did not have occasion to test my skill again until after I got married in 1932, when the garden to the house Millie and I had bought turned out to be part of a field enclosed by a wooden fence. It was over eighty foot long and quite wide so I needed help, and it was my father-in-law who came to the rescue. "First of all," he said, "you must draw a plan as to how you would like it to look."

"Well," I replied, "we would like a patio outside the dining room doors, and then a lawn with flower borders on each side, and half way up the garden a trellis arch with honeysuckle rambling over it. And beyond that it would be nice to have a couple of apple trees and space left for a vegetable patch at the top."

"Right," said my father-in-law, "let's get to work."
So we got to work, drew a plan, dug and planted and seeded and laid paths, and, with the great help of my father-in-law, we created the

lovely garden which remains, to this day, exactly as it was originally set out.

My next big horticultural venture was at the outbreak of the Second World War when I at once obtained an allotment on the edge of the green belt at the end of a nearby road, strangely named Lullington Garth. I was very enthusiastic about being an allotment holder, and year after year produced vegetables enough to keep us going all through the war, often having so many that we were able to distribute them to our neighbours and friends. (As I still do my greenhouse tomatoes and strawberries.)

After the war I had a conservatory built outside the dining room, which not only made the house warmer but also gave us another room to use. At the same time I had the coke boiler which was in the kitchen changed to gas, and when the new downstairs toilet was put in I had the new gas boiler transferred to the conservatory, keeping it warm all the year round. So, now you can see why I get geraniums *in winter,* for that is where I keep them. My love of them goes back to my working days when I saw beds of them in St James's Park. I admired them immensely and thought that I would like to have some of these myself. Therefore, once I got a heated conservatory, I was able to have geraniums not only in summer, but also to keep them in bloom during the winter months, and this I have done for many years now.

I look out of my dining room window and see a bank of them – pink and salmon and scarlet and crimson, some variegated, some tinged with the palest peach or lilac, and all set in beautiful pale green or olive green or silver-grey foliage; and every time I catch sight of them it gives me very great pleasure. The colours! And the fact that they're thriving is my reward for looking after them, which can be arduous – the tying up, the watering, the feeding, the deheading, the adjusting of the temperature; it all amounts to my loving care.

So, as I said earlier, I'm glad they're doing well. They should, I deserve it. I reckon by any standard I have done well, too. But I have striven always with the proviso that I would help other people where possible. I think I have done that, and will go on doing that.

So, even if I have retired, I'm not sitting back, oh, dear me, no. I try to help by serving on the Masonic Hospital Fund Raising Committee. I try to help individuals in whatever way I can and in whatever way they need it. I like to help. I'll drive you to the supermarket, or do the washing up. Anything you like. And when I've done my good turns, I've got all my own things to do; no little snoozes in the afternoon for me! I am gardening, as you can see; I am bowling, and attending football matches. I am doing all my own household chores, which doesn't come hard, as I'm a tidy person, though I say so myself. I am dining out, still attending Lodge meetings, and this year I gave myself a treat.

I traded in my Peugeot car and bought a Ford automatic to make driving easier, this has been a great success. The car is running well and I am very pleased with it.

My Geraniums!